THE TRAIN

THE TRAIN
A PHOTOGRAPHIC HISTORY

JONATHAN GLANCEY

CARLTON
BOOKS

THIS IS A CARLTON BOOK

This edition published in 2009 by
Carlton Books Ltd
20 Mortimer Street
London W1T 3JW

10 9 8 7 6 5 4 3 2 1

First published in 2004

Design copyright © Carlton Books Ltd
2004
Text copyright © Jonathan Glancey
2004

A CIP catalogue record for this book is
available from the British Library.

ISBN: 978 1 84732 327 9

Executive Editor: Stella Caldwell
Design: SMITH
Picture Research: Deborah Fioravanti
Production: Lisa Moore

Printed in China.

6 INTRODUCTION

Top left: A timetable from County Donegal Railways, 1956.

Top right: Timetable from the Burtonport extension, Londonderry & Lough Swilly Railway.

Bottom: Railway Map, London and South Western Railway, pre-1914.

"I am such a locomotive," wrote Augustus Welby Northmore Pugin, architect, with Charles Barry, of the Palace of Westminster, "being always flying about".

Pugin, a force of 19th-century energy running on high-pressure steam, burned himself out early; mad and dead at 40. In a firecracker career, starting at the age of 15 designing Gothic furniture for George IV at Windsor Castle, Pugin built choirs of new churches the length and breadth of England and Ireland. His designs were exported, too, either through disciples or drawings packed off on clippers as far as Australia and the United States.

He worked with a small team of dedicated builders, craftsman and decorators to achieve a vision of an England restored to what he believed to be its full, Catholic glory of the 14th century. "An assistant, sir," he barked at a visitor flabbergasted by his prodigious output of designs for churches, monasteries, houses, furniture, books, wallpaper and every last detail of the interiors of the Houses of Parliament... "Never employ one. I would kill him in a week."

The secret of this evangelizing Victorian archangel's success in building so much so quickly, aside from his innate drive and furious energy, was the train. Born eight years after Richard Trevithick, the Cornish engineer, demonstrated his first successful locomotive at the Pennydarren ironworks in south Wales, Pugin made immediate and extensive use of the first public railways as they spread their iron tentacles across a rapidly industrializing England.

This driving force behind the Victorian Gothic Revival was no enemy of the train as romantic poets like William Wordsworth or eminent critics like John Ruskin were. Pugin saw them as a reliable means of taking his message and architecture wherever a client showed willing. His journeys were extensive.

Pugin died in 1852, by which time trains and the railway had become part and parcel of everyday life in many parts of the world. They spread as fast as early steam locomotives could run. And these were often much faster than many passengers today might know, or imagine to be the case. As early as 1847, Daniel Gooch's seven-foot (and a quarter-inch) gauge Great Western Railway 4-2-2s were averaging 60mph – a mile a minute – on sections of the broad and all but level trunk route engineered by Isambard Kingdom Brunel from London Paddington to Bristol Temple Meads. These magnificent engines, which were built over many years and only finally taken out of service in 1892 when Brunel's broad gauge was replaced by the standard gauge of four feet eight-and-a-half inches, could run at 80mph. So, too, could the long-legged, big-wheeled locomotives of Thomas Crampton, taken up enthusiastically by French railways from the late 1840s. To "take a Crampton" was, for many years in France, synonymous with catching an express passenger train.

Trevithick's Pennydarren locomotive of 1804 ran at 5mph. Stephenson's *Rocket* was timed at 30mph at the Rainhill trials of 1829, a year before the opening of the Liverpool & Manchester Railway. Speed crept up inexorably and inevitably as professionals, like Pugin, and Victorian businessmen realized just how much work they could do, and how much extra wealth they could generate, by moving themselves as well as manufactured goods and mail around first Britain, and then Europe and the US, at an ever faster rate.

By the turn of the 19th century, trains in Britain, the US and Europe were able to run at up to 90mph, with many expresses timed at average speeds of 50 to 55mph. Not only that, but some of these trains had become luxurious things, equipped with dining and sleeping cars, with lavatories, barbers, electric light, decent suspension and attendants galore. Track and signalling had improved in leaps and bounds, so that trains rode faster, more smoothly and more safely than ever before.

All this had been a true revolution. Before the birth of the locomotive-hauled train, the fastest any human had been able to travel, short of falling off a mountain or church tower, was at the speed of a galloping horse, or wind-powered ship.

There were many people in 1830 who believed that their lungs, and perhaps even their rib cages, would be crushed by the unprecedented forces working on their frames, stout as well as feeble, as trains reached giddy speeds of 30mph and more. The first recorded passenger fatality was a sadder and far more obvious affair: George Huskisson, Member of Parliament for Liverpool, stepped out from his train at the gala opening of the Liverpool & Manchester to greet the Duke of Wellington, and was crushed by the *Rocket*.

More important for 19th century travellers than sheer speed was reliability. To run trains efficiently and safely, railways needed schedules. Timetables promised a clockwork railway system: as the sun would rise the next morning, so the 10 o'clock Scotch expresses would depart from London's Euston and King's Cross terminuses. It said so, in big inky type on densely packed Victorian posters. The timetable was not a work of fiction: it was a pact, a covenant, between the railways and a new travelling public. Services on a number of the new railways became so reliable that men in stove-pipe hats would set their fob-watches by them.

The railways, though, offered something more than timekeeping. Increasingly, they connected with one another, so that by 1869, for instance, it became possible to travel from one side of the US to the other by train. Today, railway lines girdle the world. For many people, they are a basic form of

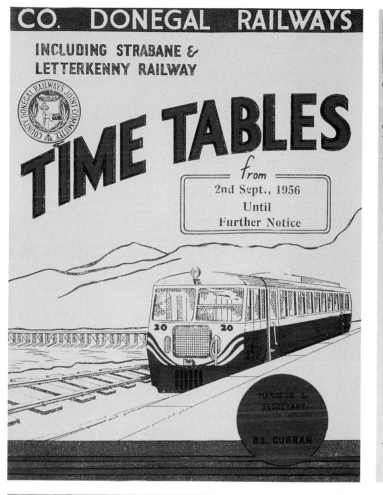

TIME TABLE

Operative on MONDAY, 27th SEPTEMBER, 1937, and thereafter until further notice.

Down Trains.		Week Days. A.M.	P.M.	P.M.
LONDONDERRY	dep.	10 0		
Gallagh Road	-	A		
Bridge End	arr.	10 11		
	dep.	10 25		
Burnfoot	-	10 30		
TOOBAN JUNC.	arr.	10 33		
Inch Road				
Fahan				
Lisfannon Golf Links				
BUNCRANA	arr.			
TOOBAN JUNC.	dep.	10 40		
Carrowen	-	10 49		
Newtoncunningham	-	11 5		
Sallybrook	-	11 21		
Manorcunningham	-	11 27		
Pluck	-	11 35		
LETTERKENNY	arr.	11 50		
	dep.	12 20	5 50	
Oldtown	-	12 24	5 54	
New Mills	-	A	A	
Foxhall	-	12 42	6 12	
Churchill	-	12 52	6 22	
Kilmacrenan	-	1 10	6 29	
Barnes Halt	-	A	A	
CREESLOUGH	arr.	1 35	7 1	
	dep.	1 40	7 7	
Dunfanaghy Road	-	1 44	7 12	
Falcarragh	-	2 12	7 40	
Cashelmagore	-	2 23	7 55	
GWEEDORE	arr.	2 43	8 10	
	dep.	2 55	8 18	
Crolly	-	3 4	8 29	
Kincasslagh Road	-	3 22	8 47	
Dungloe Road	-	3 30	8 55	
BURTONPORT	arr.	3 35	9 0	

Up Trains.		Week Days. A.M.	P.M.	P.M.	P.M.
BURTONPORT	dep.	8 30	2 0	4 15	
Dungloe Road	-	8 36	2 6	4 21	
Kincasslagh Road	-	8 41	2 12	4 27	
Crolly	-	8 56	2 29	4 44	
GWEEDORE	arr.	9 6	2 39	4 54	
	dep.	9 15	2 44	4 59	
Cashelmagore	-	9 35	3 2	5 17	
Falcarragh	-	9 46	3 12	5 27	
Dunfanaghy Road	-	10 15	3 30	5 54	
CREESLOUGH	arr.	10 20	3 43	5 59	
	dep.	10 25	3 48	6 4	
Barnes Halt	-	A			
Kilmacrenan	-	10 55	4 20	6 40	
Churchhill	-	11 5	4 20	6 46	
Foxhall	-	11 16	4 41	6 57	
New Mills	-	A		A	
Oldtown	-	11 35	4 55	7 11	
LETTERKENNY	arr.	11 40	4 58	7 14	
	dep.	12 0			
Pluck	-	12 13			
Manorcunningham	-	12 20			
Sallybrook	-	12 27			
Newtoncunningham	-	12 45			
Carrowen	-	12 55			
BUNCRANA	dep.				
Lisfannon Golf Links					
Fahan					
Inch Road					
TOOBAN JUNC.	arr.	1 5			
	dep.	1 10			
Burnfoot	-	A			
Bridge End	arr.	1 18			
	dep.	1 23			
Gallagh Road	-	A			
LONDONDERRY	arr.	1 35			

"A" Stops to pick up passengers if required; also to set down passengers on notice being given to Guard at previous stop.

N.B.—See separate Timetable for full particulars of the Company's Omnibus Services.

JAS. WHYTE, Manager & Secretary.

Express Corridor Luncheon & Dining Trains between London & Bournemouth & the West of England.

L.S.W.R. Co. Fast Twin Screw Steamers between Southampton & the Channel Islands Havre, Honfleur, St. Malo & Cherbourg in connection with express trains from all parts.

1881 – A CARLOAD OF NAVEL ORANGES FROM _____

Top: Unloading cider apples.

Bottom left: Stylized giant oranges by Southern Pacific, 1909.

Bottom right: Lumber carried by a classic American wood-burning locomotive.

transport; to others a luxury or, in the case of the preserved historic railways of the world, a happy indulgence.

The impact of the railways was instant – and astonishing. The train was one of the great step-changes in the way humans have ordered their lives: their impact was as great as that of the invention of writing, the wheel, the stirrup, moveable type, inoculation and, later on, automobiles, aircraft and the internet. All these things have given us reasons, and prompted us, to move ever more freely across our world, to make connections where there were none before.

In today's terms, the railway was a kind of solid World Wide Web. It does seem remarkable that within 40 years of the first express trains, it was possible to travel across the US in some comfort in just four days, from Montreal to New York in one, and from London to Edinburgh in 10 hours. Within this same time frame, the world's first underground railway – the Metropolitan from Paddington to Farringdon, London, 1863 – had opened for smoky business, and popular excursion trains were taking thousands of factory and farm workers, many of whom had never travelled more than 10 miles from their homes, on jaunts to events like the Great Exhibition in Hyde Park, London, 1851, or to the seaside.

The remarkable growth of passenger traffic was one thing; that of goods or freight, another. Before the Liverpool & Manchester, the prime purpose of the emerging railways was shouldering tons of iron, coal and other raw materials and basic goods from mines to factories or points of distribution. In fact, wagons on rails, either pushed by hand or pulled by horses, had been around for a very long time. The Romans had used them, and they were a feature of mines in various parts of Europe for hundreds of years before Trevithick showed that steam power could be used to do the work of both men and horses. The railway was not a wholly new idea but the locomotive was.

And no wonder the railway locomotive attracted so many fans. In the steam locomotive, Trevithick and his successors created a machine that appeared to be alive. Of course, it must have been frightening, and not just to horses, in its early years. But, very soon, the steam locomotive became a highly regarded and much loved part of the new industrial landscape. The train was not just useful, it was a marvellous thing in its own right. It was not long before artists attempted to represent its elemental beauty, its promise of relentless, rhythmic speed and pluming, pulsating power.

Joseph Mallord William Turner's "Rain, Speed and Steam", depicting a Gooch Great Western 4-2-2 racing across a viaduct between Paddington and Reading, was a brilliant evocation of the magical quality of a steam train in full flight;

part dragon, part factory furnace, a fiery herald of the burgeoning industrial world, at once both frightening and marvellous. Turner's scurrying locomotive was a machine that tore at Victorian emotions. Was it a force for good or evil?

Within decades, romantics and medieval revivalists would be decrying the train, and especially the smoking steam locomotive – it had made life too fast, too dirty, too in hock to rigid timetables. Such critics were about to become a tiny minority. True, the train encouraged towns and cities to grow like Topsy, now that it was possible to commute to work; true, city air was laced with sulphur, and noble edifices smeared with soot. But a new beauty, as well as new efficiency, had been born.

Was there a golden age of the railway? There probably was, some time perhaps between 1900 and 1920 before the car got its grip on the public imagination, and on modest purses. Between these years, railways were at their peak in terms of the sheer number and diversity of lines constructed. Carriages, even Third Class if you rode railways like the Midland from Manchester and Derby down to the spectacular Gothic Revival station and hotel at St Pancras from the 1870s, were grand. Freight trains moved much of the land-based economy throughout the developed and developing world. Mechanical engineering had matured, along with materials technology, and locomotives were often refined and beautiful things. Johnson's elegant Midland Railway Singles (4-2-2) of 1882, for example, were not only fast, smooth and reliable, they also hid their mechanical workings and underpinnings from crews, passengers and shed staff alike. Wondrous things, they would have appeared to glide along, a haze of steam at the top of their tall chimneys, their rich maroon paintwork gleaming. It was a remarkable feat of seamless engineering; a machine worked by pistons, cranks, eccentrics – a symphony of reciprocating parts – that appeared to have no moving parts at all, aside that is from its great, Penny Farthing driving wheels.

This was a very British preoccupation, an elegant denial of the nature and workings of industrialism. It reminds me of the story of John Ruskin's honeymoon: an admirer of chaste marble statues of women, he was rather aghast to discover that his attractive young wife, Effie, had pubic hair and bled. The Johnson single was as chaste as a railway locomotive, or a Victorian art critic, could be.

In France, locomotive engineers allowed everything to hang out; their engines were voluptuaries of domes and tubes, a mass of unfathomable plumbing, and all of it on display like the workings of the Pompidou Centre

Right: Streamlining, before and
after. Pennsylvania RR K4 Pacifics
and Raymond Loewy, an industrial
designer, 1936.

in Paris designed by Richard Rogers and Renzo Piano in the 1970s. This was
much the same aesthetic at play; the vital parts of engines and buildings
were worthy of public display.

Many European locomotives were much like this; so, too, their distant US
cousins, unless they were streamlined. However, the big difference with
American locomotives, from early on, was their massive and muscular scale.

There were really only four major schools of locomotive design: US or North
American, British, French and German. Most locomotives encountered in the
world were derived from one of these schools. In fact, most of the steam
locomotives built between 1830 and 1990 were simple, rugged, two-cylinder
machines that performed sterling service in North and South America, Europe,
Asia, Africa and Australasia.

But we all have our preferences, our own favourite locomotives, and our
own "golden ages". Mine are for railways of a later period. While all trains
interest me, I have a quiet passion for the late-flowering steam era, when
locomotive engineers like Paul Kiefer on the New York Central in the US, and
Andre Chapelon on the SNCF (the French state railways), were pushing
steam technology to new and extreme limits, even as diesels and electrics
snapped at their fast-spinning axles.

Both engineers produced legendary locomotives that I wish I could have
seen in action. The NYC Niagara S-1 class 4-8-4 of 1945 was a wondrous work of
steam engineering. These brute beauties could generate 6,650ihp (indicated
horsepower, the power produced in the locomotive's cylinders) at 85mph; they
could top 100mph with 1,000-ton trains; they could run up to 28,000 miles a
month with the help of fully automated depots. Painted glossy black, equipped
with air horns as well as bell and steam whistle, they must have made a
heart-quickening sight, and sound, as they thundered along the Hudson Valley
at the head of massive Pullman sleepers or fast freight trains.

Sadly, these mighty machines, although proven to be as economical to run as
the latest diesels, went the way of steam railway traction throughout the US in
the 1950s: it was seen to be dirty and old-fashioned. None is preserved. If I had
the money, I would get one built, perhaps in one of the surviving locomotive
works in China before the Chinese forget the knack of steam engineering.

Or I would invest my theoretical millions in reconstructing André Chapelon's
peerless 242A1 three-cylinder compound 4-8-4 of 1946. Probably, the most
efficient of all steam railway locomotives to date, 242A1 weighed about half as
much as a two-cylinder Niagara, but could produce up to 5,500ihp, and clear
100mph. She was designed to show that a modern steam locomotive could run

to the latest electric timetables and, like an electric locomotive, accelerate
rapidly and maintain high speeds consistently uphill and down. On trial, this
great and solitary locomotive bettered the scintillating new electric schedules,
much to the chagrin of SNCF management, who wanted to oust steam for good.
She was scrapped, sadly, shortly after being taken out of service in 1960.

Just as sad is the fact that Chapelon's earlier 240P 4-8-0 compounds were all
scrapped, too. These compact and pugnacious machines weighing just 109 tons
could produce 4,000ihp, and 3,400dbhp (drawbar horsepower, or the power a
locomotive has to pull its train after subtracting the power it needs to move
itself) more or less continuously. Few diesel locomotives have ever been able to
match their efficiency; Chapelon was designing steam engines to take on the
electrics that would finally oust them on the French railways in the early 1970s.

Those fine electrics were eventually to run at 200km/h in everyday service;
Chapelon had attempted to beat them to it. From the late 1940s, he proposed a
new series of steam locomotives for the SNCF, including a compound 4-6-4 for
200km/h passenger services and a 120km/h 6,000ihp 2-10-4 for fast freight.
They would have been every bit as exhilarating to experience in action as
Kiefer's Niagaras or their rivals, the almost dream-like Pennsylvania Railroad
T-series 4-4-4-4s, but the SNCF refused to support Chapelon's visionary project.
For them, as for railway management through much of the world in the 1950s,
steam was considered not so much inefficient compared with diesel and
electric fashion, but part of an old order that must give way to new.

The locomotive is, of course, only one part of the train, but it is its heart and
soul, and the most spectacular part of the ensemble. Snake-like 300km/h EMUs
(electric multiple units) of 21st century railways are impressive, but very
different machines. A great deal of care went into their design, and yet Jack
Cooper, the British-born industrial designer who trained with Raymond Loewy
– a master of publicity who designed sensational streamlined casings for
Pennsylvania Railroad 4-6-2s and its solitary 6-4-4-6 express passenger
locomotive in the 1930s – was specifically called on to draw up a "train that
didn't look like a train" when commissioned to shape the SNCF's bright orange
TGVs. Together with the Japanese National Railways' Shinkansen bullet trains
before them, and many ultra-fast trains since, TGVs are a kind of aircraft
without wings on tracks. It might be said of them, by traditionalists, "C'est
magnifique, mais c'est ne pas le train." They are, of course, very fine trains,
but very different, and an abrupt change, from what had gone before.

The aesthetic of the steam locomotive had developed slowly. What had
begun with Trevithick, Hedley and Stephenson as a kind of steam pump or giant

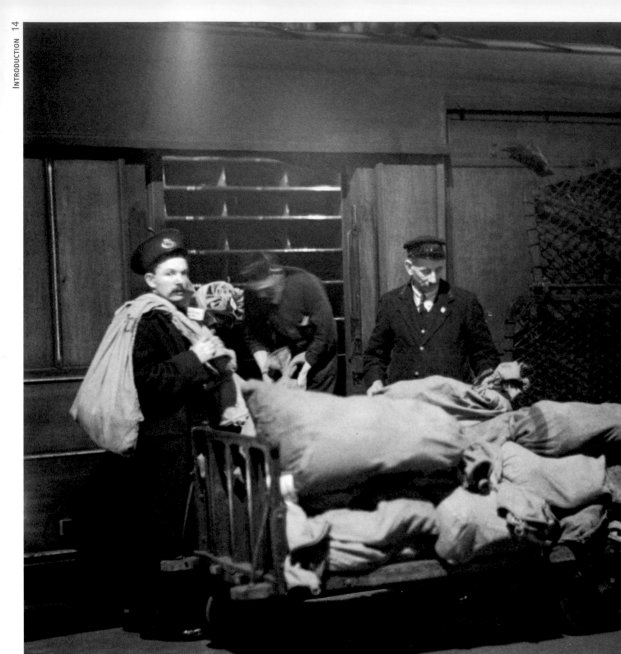

kettle on wheels slowly transformed into the classic Stephensonian locomotive, with its long, multi-tubed boiler resting on top of wheels driven by a reciprocating engine, with cylinders and valves up front, exhaust drawn through a chimney on top of a smokebox directly above the cylinders.

Despite many experiments over the decades to alter or even revolutionize this layout – take a look at Oliver Bulleid's Leader 0-6-6-0 diesel lookalike for the Southern Region of British Railways (p165) – the last, and many of the best, steam locomotives never lost the basic architecture established by Stephenson with his early locomotives for the Liverpool & Manchester.

Shape apart, one of the endearing and enduring features of steam locomotives is not the way they successfully fuse together the four ancient elements – earth (in the guise of iron, steel, copper, brass, bronze, coal and oil), air, fire and water – but the wonderful insistent noise they make, the universally popular song they sing.

It is this sound that has nursed many generations of children to sleep at night; it is a sound that delights railways enthusiasts, and one that has haunted the imaginations of musicians. Whether classical, jazz, boogie-woogie, blues, country or pop, the steam locomotive has played its influential part.

In an interview in 1923, the Swiss-born French composer Arthur Honegger said, "I have always had a passionate liking for locomotives; for me they are living things and I love them as others love women or horses." Honegger's dissonant orchestral masterpiece "Pacific 231" (1923) is a translation into musical terms of the composer's love of the steam locomotive.

Others, like the English composer Benjamin Britten, caught the spirit and excitement of a great steam train picking up speed and racing for home. The music Britten wrote to accompany W H Auden's poem in the GPO Film Unit's *Night Mail* (1936) cannot be heard without the sight of the LMS Royal Scot 4-6-0 *Seaforth Highlander* galloping down from Shap towards Carlisle and the Scottish border at the head of the famous West Coast Postal; it springs to mind as surely as heather does from those northern English and lowland Scottish fells.

Nor can it be heard without Auden's poem rattling in the mind's ear, for this, too, captures perfectly the rhythm of a steam locomotive, at first climbing hard:

This is the Night Mail crossing the border
Bringing the cheque and the postal order...

Auden conjures the rhythmic punch of pistons pounding in and out of hard-worked cylinders...

And then streaking down hill:

Letters for the rich, letters for the poor,
The shop at the corner and the girl next door ...

Here you can hear the diddle-dee-dum, diddle-de dee clatter of a train flying down a gradient in the days when main-line tracks were jointed rather than continuously welded.

Many 19th- and 20th-century composers were either overt railway enthusiasts, and attempted to orchestrate impressions of steam locomotives at work, or they were musicians fascinated by the compelling chant of locomotives whether setting out heroically from stations or streaking through landscapes with a lively clickety-clack clatter of train wheels behind them.

You can, should you want to, hear trains at work in one form or another in Sibelius's *Night Ride and Sunrise*, the opening of Bruckner's Fourth Symphony, the scherzo from Dvorak's D-minor symphony, Stravinsky's *The Rite of Spring* and Gershwin's *Rhapsody in Blue*.

Elmer Bernstein's *Toccatta for Toy Trains* (1956), written for an enchanting short film by the US designers Charles and Ray Eames, evokes the spirit of old-time steam railroading delightfully. Michael Nyman's insistent MGV (Musique à Grande Vitesse), commissioned to mark the opening of the TGV Nord service (1993), captures, and then relentlessly abstracts and sustains, the persistent, smooth rhythm of one of these super-fast electric trains.

The blues were often inspired by the sight and sound of lonesome trains that promised to take black cotton plantation workers north to Chicago, to new jobs and a new life. Jimi Hendrix's "I Hear My Train a Comin'" is a magnificent, late-flowering blues masterpiece that captures the yearning for that train to arrive.

Meade Lux Lewis's "Honky Tonk Trains Blues" (1926) is fine, fast boogie-woogie piano romp that sizzles like a locomotive on a hot, fast run. You imagine that there must have been a-reelin' and a-rockin' cocktail bar on board Lux Lewis's train.

Pop music abounds in train songs, from the introspective like Simon and Garfunkel's "Homeward Bound", to the upbeat like the Monkees' "Last Train to Clarksville".

Poets, too, have been caught by the rhythm of the steam train, and its quiet moments. Sterling Plumpp, the blues poet and professor of African-American Literature at Chicago University, writes brilliantly about the lure of trains steaming north from Mississippi and Louisiana for poor, rural blacks. He was

Right: Preserved Princess
Coronation Pacific, the 46229
Duchess of Hamilton, on the
Settle and Carlisle route, Cumbria,
in 1983.

one of them, brought up on a plantation; whenever he heard or saw a train pass, he would think of the life that he might have if only he could climb aboard one of those trains. He did.

John Betjeman (1906–84), the late English Poet Laureate, caught the sight and sound of railways in numerous poems. Edward Thomas (1878–1917), an English poet killed in Flanders in the First World War, found exactly the right words to describe the strange and heightened feelings that come when a steam train pulls up in the middle of nowhere and passengers wait expectantly, as it simmers impatiently, to hear it whistle, hiss and puff once again:

Yes, I remember Adlestrop
Because one afternoon of heat
The express train drew up there unwontedly
The steam hissed, someone cleared his throat
No one went and no one came on the bare platform
What I remember is Adlestrop, only the name

All trains have the power to lull passengers to sleep because of the quieting rhythm of steel wheels rolling along steel tracks, the muffled ring of crossing bells, the rumbles under bridges and over girders. It is particularly comforting to sleep behind a steam locomotive, with its compulsive chant and mournful cry penetrating rail-induced dreams. Wonderful, too, of course, to wake up and watch plumes of steam trailing along and over the train as night gives way to day in some unknown landscape and the attendant at the end of the car prepares breakfast.

The steam locomotive is a machine, but it has a warm as well as a musical heart. I enjoyed this warmth very much in February 2003 when I was working, as a driver and fireman, on the PKP (Polish State Railways) lines from Wolsztyn to Lezno and Poznan. The morning I arrived for duty on the 0416 fast stopping commuter train to Poznan, the town was deep under snow and the temperature was −20°C, a morning when most sane people would turn over in bed and sleep right through the alarm. Yet once on board Ol-49 69, all was well with the railway world. The grate of this no-nonsense 1950s 2-6-2 was blazing; sausages, bread rolls and bottles of tea were already warming through on the backplate of the boiler. Once on the move, in clouds of superheated steam, who cared about the cold?

The times I have spent on the footplates of steam locomotives have been some of the most thrilling and fulfilling of my life. As a little boy, I dreamed of riding the footplate of a Stanier Princess Coronation Pacific even more than I did of flying a Spitfire or driving a D-Type Jaguar. These handsome machines were the most powerful steam locomotives to run in Britain: they were fast, free steaming, reliable and much respected. In their streamlined youth, in striking blue and white or red and gold stripes, they ran the *Coronation Scot* from Euston to Glasgow. When I was born, they were still in charge of the heaviest Scottish expresses, pounding up the grades from London with 16-car sleepers, pulling small towns behind them through northern towns still governed by heavy industry, and across the sheep-studded hills of Shap and Beattock. They tackled these herculean tasks, if not with disdain, then with consummate ease.

In 1990, I spent a day learning to drive Coronation 46229 *Duchess of Hamilton*, in the snow, between Loughborough and Leicester. Getting this mighty Pacific to start her 12-coach train without slipping on the icy tracks was a proud achievement.

The next year, I helped prepare *Duchess of Hamilton* early one morning for a Pullman car special running from Leeds to Carlisle and back over the daunting and magnificent Settle and Carlisle Route. Removing cork plugs from her axle boxes to top these up with oil, in misty darkness while the boiler hummed above me, was a daunting experience and a reminder that, while Stanier's masterpiece was a superb machine, labour at the time of her building had been cheap. If she had been an American locomotive, oil would have been fed automatically to her axle boxes. But this, I mused, was a real Duchess above me; she needed and enjoyed a large complement of respectful servants to attend her every need.

Out on the road, this beautifully preserved locomotive, owned for the nation by the National Railway Museum, York, was mistress of her task. She rode like one of the 12 Pullman carriages behind her. At speed — and we did run fast — she ran as sweetly as some gigantic sewing machine. Only when we attacked the demanding gradients along the route did the *Duchess* speak with aristocratic authority. The hissing of steam from her Ross pop-safety valves, pressed to 250 pounds per square inch, the volcanic pounding of exhaust steam hurtling high from her double chimney, the occasional slip of her 6ft 9in driving wheels on wet rails… these things stirred the emotions as well as drove trainful of enthusiasts besotted by their *Duchess* to Carlisle.

I was elated but, on reflection, sad that my own country is now all but unable to build a railway locomotive at all, much less a magnificent machine like this 3,300hp Pacific. I think of all the skills for designing, building, running

and servicing her, of the huge respect she won from railway staff and passengers alike, of how she was photographed like one of today's "celebrities" and of what pleasure she had given to so many people over so many years.

When *Duchess of Hamilton* was built, in 1938, Britain's railways were in private hands. But there were just four major regional railways, and they owned and operated trains and track. Their directors, managers and engineers believed in them. They were enthusiasts of one sort or another who wanted their railway to be the best.

I knew, almost instinctively, that this love of steam railways in daily service was fading fast when I got my very first Ian Allan *Locospotter's Guide*, to the motive power of British Railways' London Midland Region. Main-line steam was on the way out in Britain. I was lucky enough to see and ride behind some of the very last. There were trips made, nipping off rigger at school, on the semi fast trains that ran from Marylebone, usually behind ex-LMS Stanier class 5 4-6-0s, the Jeep of Britain's post-war railways, running alongside and overtaking the electric Underground trains of London Transport's Bakerloo and Metropolitan lines. These steam trains seemed to be running in a parallel and almost ghostly universe at the time.

There were runs to Southampton Docks behind Bulleid West Country and Battle of Britain light Pacifics. There were trips to Lancashire to see the very last main-line steam trains hauled by Stanier class 5s, 8F 2-8-0s, and the, by then, solitary British Railways' Britannia Pacific 70013 *Oliver Cromwell*.

These journeys were made while digesting a diet of railway books and magazines. I devoured those by Cecil J Allen and O S Nock, two meticulous railway historians, and professional engineers, whose speciality was recording runs in minute detail with stopwatches from train windows and locomotive footplates. Their sense of accuracy and fair play meant that I learned early on that just as schoolboys exaggerate the top speeds of the cars they admired (thinking, for example, that because their father's Austin A60's speedometer read up to 90mph that this hard-pressed minor civil servant on wheels could actually reach such a speed), so over-enthusiastic or partisan railway enthusiasts often exaggerated the speed of favourite trains.

Allen, a fierce and puritanical fellow whose autobiography is entitled *Two Million Miles of Train Travel* taught me that it was very unlikely that the Great Western Railways 4-4-0 3440 *City of Truro* ran at 102.3mph between Bristol and Exeter in 1904, becoming the first locomotive to better 100mph. The top speed was more likely to have been about 92mph. Equally, 4472 *Flying Scotsman*, the Gresley LNER A1 Pacific (p39) that was meant to have reached a more certain

100mph in 1934 down Stoke Bank between Grantham and Peterborough, was, in all likelihood, doing no more than 97 or 98mph.

The point about this strict accord with the truth is that trains and railways were measurable things, and increasingly the stuff of scientific and tested, rather than purely pragmatic, engineering. It did their development no good if we did not know the exact truth about any particular train or locomotive's ability to perform. Wild claims from the US – among them that 999, a showcase Atlantic 4-4-2 built jointly by the Baltimore & Ohio and New York Central Railroads, ran at 112.5mph in 1893 – undermined this notion of scientific truth and true progress.

Later, I learned that Stanier's Coronation Pacific 6220 ran at a maximum speed of 112.5mph on a famous press run in 1937 (p42), and not 114mph as the LMS press office claimed at the time, and that, horror of horrors, Gresley's A4 Pacific 4468 *Mallard* (p46) may not have peaked at 126mph, to claim the world record for steam in 1938, but almost certainly topped 124.5mph, or 201km/h, the same speed as the streamlined Deutsche Reichsbahn 4-6-4 05 002 (p47) reached between Hamburg and Berlin in 1936.

The LMS wanted that extra 1.5mph to beat the LNER's existing record of 113mph and, a year later, the LNER wanted the same extra speed to beat the DR record. That these forays remain a matter of superheated debate, some 70 years on, shows just how passionate enthusiasts are about their favourite locomotives and railways.

What I learned as I grew up and my love of railways – and the steam locomotive in particular – broadened was that all railways were of interest. A knowledge of railway history, like that of architectural history, allowed me to read the development of the modern world in a way that encouraged me to travel as well as to read widely.

And, as I did so, I faced the fact that railways were not always quite as innocent as I had imagined them to be. My books, and all those logs of runs by Nock and Allen, by Church of England vicars and locomotive-besotted French aristocrats like Baron Viollet, had presented me with a world in which progress was not only desirable but also inevitable. A Great Western Churchward Saint 4-6-0 led to the Churchward Saint, Collett Castle and Collett King, each locomotive faster and more powerful than its predecessor. Steam gave way to diesel, while electric traction triumphed in the end.

The train, it seemed, was a wholly benevolent force, forever cutting five minutes off a journey here, raising speeds by 10mph there, as the 19th and 20th centuries progressed. But there was a dark side to trains, after all. In

Right: Father and son refugees
travel by train after border clashes
with China. Tezpur, India, 1962.

Nazi Germany, a perverted use of science saw otherwise robust and dignified Deutsche Reichsbahn 2-10-0s taking Jews to death camps in Germany and Poland. When we were choosing the photographs for this book, we decided not to show yet another dismal and degrading image of the fake jolly old world German station built in front of the concentration camp at Auschwitz. Instead, we opted for redemption, and show a picture of survivors from one of these dreadful places returning home by one of the very same trains that took them towards what must have seemed a certain death until the Allied victory in 1945.

The train itself is innocent, but, like the Boeing airliners hijacked by Al Qaeda terrorists on September 11, 2001, its technology can be pressed into a truly godless service.

Trains have also carried many millions of thumbs-up young soldiers, larking about for the camera as they departed stations across the world, to premature and horrid deaths. The story of the Thai-Burmese railway (p228), built by slave labour by the Japanese in the Second World War, beggars belief.

Equally, trains took children safely away from European cities during the Second World War as bombs rained down on their homes. Trains have long brought loved ones back. Trains have mapped and mirrored our lives — emotional, political and warring — for 200 years. They have been special tools that have served us for richer, for poorer, in sickness, health, war and peace.

Progress, as I learned, did not always go smoothly. In the early years of railway development, greedy speculation and the construction of far too many competing lines led to closures and bankruptcies galore. Shoddy workmanship, or poor engineering, led to countless avoidable accidents, to bridges collapsing (p110) and, in the case of the perversely shambolic Schull & Skibbereen narrow-gauge railway in southern Ireland (p145), to locomotives unable to move themselves let alone their trains.

Three cases of perverse failure come to mind, one that began in the mid-1950s, one from my early childhood and one from recent political history. In 1955, British Railways announced its Modernization Plan. Away with soot and cinders. In with a brave new world of US-style diesel and French-style electric trains; in with Modern architecture and slimmed-down rural services. But when BR managers and motive power engineers began to specify the new diesels, they got it very wrong. Instead of researching and developing a few powerful, fast, reliable and forward-looking types, they bought more dogs' breakfasts than even a bulldog would care for.

Fleets of fast, much-liked and well-proven steam Pacifics, refined and developed over decades, gave way to slower, less powerful and unreliable

diesel-electrics brought pretty much off-the-shelf. A BR design panel tried its best to make them look more modern than the late 1930s American diesels that most of them were, although they were not nearly as well built. There were dozens of new types of diesels, very few of them any good. They had to be looked after by steam locomotives, which were stationed up and down main lines to rescue their trains, and regain time, when the diesels gave up the ghost. This was an Indian summer for steam enthusiasts recording spirited runs by British Pacifics as they made up time lost by the new diesels, but a disaster for Britain's railways. For just as the post-war consumer economy was booming and the British could afford to buy and run cars, and just as the first motorways opened and first inter-city jets took to the air, the railways invested in a form of motive power that was unable to match the best steam performances of the 1930s, let alone the 1950s and 1960s.

It took British Railways several years to sort out this mess. It had lost a decade in terms of progress and very many passengers because of its management's dumb insistence that poor-performing new diesels were the thing to have because they appeared to be modern. BR management's loathing of the steam locomotive at the time can hardly be imagined today, now that a younger generation enjoys the sight of steam specials running alongside high-speed modern electrics.

This hatred of steam, and the determination to be modern whatever the cost to the railways, led to an appalling deterioration of many passenger services in the 1960s. Steam locomotives would be turned out for duty, unlike their siblings in France, East and West Germany, Poland, South Africa, India and the Soviet Union, in ramshackle condition. Important express trains would be run by filthy locomotives, leaking steam from every pipe and gland, with a hard-pressed crew expected to make the best of a bad job.

I remember reading in the back pages of the *Railway Magazine*, when I was expected to be reading *The Famous Five*, *Milly Molly Mandy* or Hilaire Belloc's *Bad Book of Beasts*, a note to the effect that a winter run on one of the semi-fasts from Marylebone to Nottingham Victoria had been composed of two unheated non-corridor coaches and an 8F 2-8-0 designed to haul freight trains at 50mph. This steam line closed soon afterwards, much to the glee of railway management. The few passengers left got behind the wheels of their cars.

In 1963, Dr Richard Beeching, chairman of British Railways, announced his infamous report that sounded the death knell for many rural branch lines in Britain. When I got hear about Beeching and his fearful report, I imagined him to be a medical doctor brought in to amputate the limbs of favourite

Left: Modern diesel freight power.
BNSF trains snake through the
Colorado landscape.

railways. How useful so many of the lines he closed would be today; management of his day was in awe of the car and gave in to it.

This, though, was not nearly as great a crime as the utterly bodged and wilfully childish privatization of Britain's main line railways in 1997. The aim of a generation of business-crazy Tory and New Labour politicians was to break the state railway into a number of rival fiefdoms run by businessmen whose primary interest was personal gain rather than public duty or a love of railways.

The very politicians who have done their best to undermine Britain's railways, during a time when railways have been doing so brilliantly well in France, Spain, Italy, Germany and in much else of Europe, had benefited hugely from being brought up in a welfare state. Now, in an act of surly and petulant patricide, they wanted to destroy the world that had done so much for them. By 2004, Britain's railways were in a sorry state. There were increasing calls for the railways to be taken back into state hands and run by managers who cared about them.

Elsewhere in the world, railways are largely in state hands or run by companies who have responsibility for both track and trains. The important thing, not understood by politicians in Britain but by every child who has ever been given a model railway for Christmas, is that railways are a system, a network, and need to be run as whole.

This is particularly true now that advanced technology, and great speeds, mean that modern railways are expensive and demanding operations, although offering huge ecological benefits over cars and planes.

In the US, the changeover to diesel traction and the decline of passenger traffic in the 1950s was caused by different reasons. American steam locomotives were developed to a remarkable degree. In the 1940s, mile-long Union Pacific freight trains were running at 70-80mph behind the railroad's Big Boy 4-8-8-4s. There were many Pacific and 4-8-4 locomotives capable of running 1,000-ton passenger trains at 100mph on level track. Mechanization of motive power depots was impressive. The final generation of US steam locomotives could match the latest General Motors' diesels, cent for cent.

The reason the diesel lobby won is severalfold. Railway management was not necessarily taken with the new diesels. But General Motors, unlike old-fashioned steam locomotive manufacturers, was run on modern lines with slick sales teams and the promise of alluring back-up programmes. GM was God in many quarters of US business and politics; the burgeoning giant was on a roll.

Although its individual diesel-electric units were much less powerful than the steam locomotives they replaced, they could be coupled together in series to get the horsepower needed to get their trains running, and these were operated by a single crew. They were less specialized than their steam counterparts, handling a greater variety of trains. They could accelerate more quickly, although were rarely as fast at the top end as steam, and they could be started at the turn of a key.

A number of railroads like the Norfolk & Western stayed loyal to steam, developing some of the most efficient, powerful and rapid steam railway locomotives. As the steam locomotive industry closed down around them, though, and parts were harder to get, the writing was on the wall. Steam had lost.

But so had the passenger railway in the US. By 1957, for the first time, more people flew than travelled by train. The sheer scale of the US allowed the airlines to win out, even though the very best First Class flight in a Boeing 747 or 777 today cannot compare with the elegance, luxury, space and sheer style of the New York Central's *Twentieth Century Limited* in its heyday. Only after the events of September 11, 2001, did Americans begin thinking seriously of taking the long-distance train again, by which time most had gone.

Throughout the rest of the world, modernization of the railways has moved at a greater or lesser extent. Western Europe and Japan have proved that the train can beat aircraft hands down over distances of as much as 500 miles. The SNCF's TGVs effectively ended passenger air traffic between Paris and Lyon. Now the train is competitive from Paris to Marseilles. The staggeringly frequent Shinkansen trains of the Japanese railways have brought about nothing less than a revolution in public transport, putting the car in its proper place – plaything, status symbol, runabout – and encouraging jets to fly between countries rather than within them.

In China, the last hardy and handsome 3,500ihp QJ 2-10-2s work some of the People's Republic's most recently built and demanding lines, carrying prodigious quantities of raw material to build a new China that will witness their own impending demise.

In Russia, the train remains a wonderful way to travel. The Rossiya Trans-Siberian Express is only one of many long-distance trains in which meals change along the line as often as local food and customs do.

In India, the train is a way of life. In the US and Canada, railway freight traffic is booming. In Australia, there has been much excitement over the newly opened line from Alice Springs to Darwin, making it possible to ride a train from north to south coast.

From point to point overland, the train remains the most civilized way to

Right: Boldly going where no train has gone before: the Ghan on its way, for the first time, from Adelaide to Darwin via Alice Springs, 2004.

travel quickly, although it might not seem like this to commuters. Its revival seems assured, especially in an environmentally concerned age.

I hope you like this book. It is a snapshot album of the train as it emerged from the Industrial Revolution in Britain, and spread around the world. It shows how the train affected so much in our lives; how it encouraged new forms of engineering; how it challenged designers and architects; how it changed the shape and pace of our cities; how it learned to reinvent itself at the end of the 20th century. We see the train as political tool, as hostage of war, as film star, and as eccentric plaything, too. When I look at these pictures, I wish I could have ridden not just the great trains of the world as they were years ago, but also some of the railway world's delightfully eccentric byways.

I have walked the 50 miles or so of the long-abandoned, and ill-fated, Burtonport extension of the Londonderry and Lough Swilly Railway in Northern Ireland. It winds through high, deserted and bog-infested country on its way from Derry to a tiny, Atlantic coast, fishing port. It bore few passengers and a disappointing amount of freight, yet it boasted the biggest narrow-gauge locomotives in the British Isles, a handsome brood of 4-8-0 tender locomotives and 4-8-4 tanks. What was the point of building such an ambitious railway and such grand locomotives? Railwaymania, I suppose. As this book shows, railways got almost everywhere, across deserts, up and through mountains, and to the loneliest villages, the most isolated ports.

You will have your own favourite railways, locomotives and trains. The choice is huge, and there are so many missing here which we would have liked to include. But, fortunately, the literature on world railways is encyclopaedic; my own railway library is beginning to demand a building of its own. Here, I can find the endless technical minutiae that I can only allude to in this book – dates of openings and closures, names and speeds of trains, biographies of locomotive engineers, boiler pressures, cylinder bore diameters, menus from the dining cars of favourite historic trains. How about "Roast Prime Ribs of Beef, Au Jus", or "Broiled Shrewsbury Squab, Guava Jelly, Timbale of Wild Rice, Creamed Wax Beans, O'Brien Potatoes" from the dinner menu – $1.75 including appetiser, starter, entrée, pudding or cheese, tea or coffee – aboard the 1938, steam-hauled *20th Century Limited*? Or a Martini cocktail for 40 cents?

For those who love the steam locomotive, it is encouraging to see how experienced engineers like David Wardale (p171) are designing a new generation of machine aimed at hauling tourist, enthusiast and business specials, at a maximum speed of 200km/h, and keeping steam alive in the long term.

For those who love railways in general, their future seems secure, except in the country that invented them. It is sad when a whole country, like Paraguay or Togo, abandons its entire railway system, or to look up today's New York–Chicago passenger service via the path of the *Twentieth Century Limited* and to find just one through-train taking 18 hours 20 minutes for a journey that took 16 hours in much greater style in 1938; in 1948, there were 10 through-trains each day. There is the strange case of Africa, where once magnificent systems, like the East African Railways serving today's Kenya, Uganda and Tanzania, are a shadow of their former selves, as sadly are the once prosperous and forward-looking railways of today's Zimbabwe and South Africa. Many African countries have never built railways, among them Chad, Niger, Liberia, Gambia, Somalia, Rwanda and the Central African Republic.

But the Italian-built Eritrean state railway (p149) is re-opening in East Africa, and the Trans-Jordan Railway based in Amman is getting slowly back on track and harbours ambitious plans for a line across the desert to Baghdad. There are new lines in Russia, China (p56) and the Welsh highlands (p150).

In the fields of architecture and engineering, there have been great strides made in recent years. The new stations along the TGV line south to Marseilles are of a very high order, as is the dramatic Lyon-Satalas station serving Lyon airport and designed by the world-famous Spanish architect-engineer, Santiago Calatrava.

The one thing missing in many trains today is the kind of spacious and luxurious accommodation once offered by railways throughout the world. Far too many trains are now composed of overbright, fluorescent-lit stock, kitted out in garish fabrics, and blighted by interminable public address announcements, the insistent tss-tss of personal stereos and wilfully loud telephone monologues delivered over mobile phones. These things came to pass in the developed world when the railways and the train lost some of their appeal to well-heeled travellers between the 1950s and 1990s.

Today, the railways have the chance to be as well designed and as dynamic as they ever were, to be a vital ingredient of economic and cultural success in the 21st century just as they were for restless and peripatetic architects like Augustus Pugin in the 19th century. Some of us will always long for the smell of hot oil and the rhythmic music of the steam locomotive, but will forgive the railways this great loss if they deliver the style, quality and quantity of services that will get people out of their cars, and goods out of lorries – and both out of planes – and on to rails running forever faster than fairies, faster than witches into a new golden era.

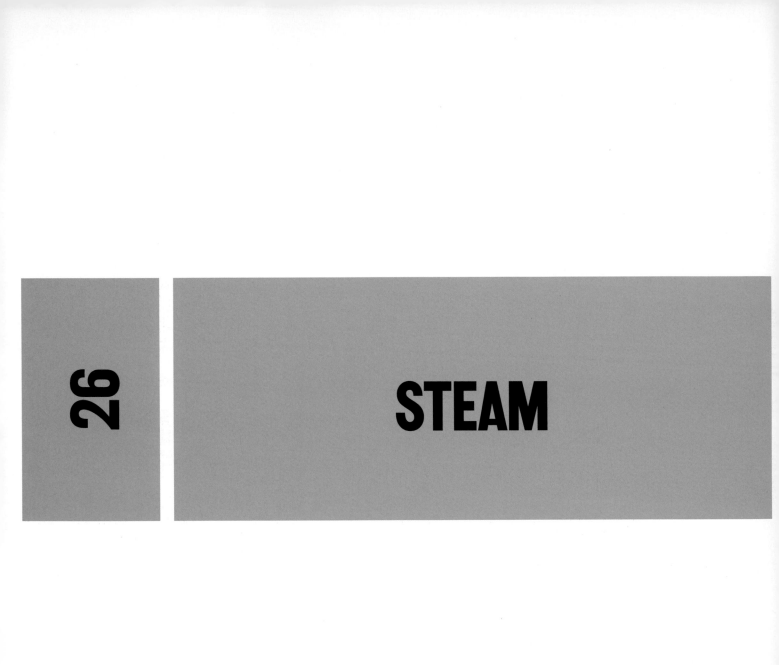

26

STEAM

Steam locomotives are a common language. In travels around the world, I have been delighted by the ways in which a shared passion for steam can cut through cultural barriers. Whether on the footplate of a QJ 2-10-2 climbing a mountain pass in a blizzard through Inner Mongolia, or whistling through rural, early morning Poland at the controls of a PKP 2-6-2 in deepest winter, there has been no need to speak Mongolian or Polish, much less the Queen's, or George Stephenson's, English.

Steam men – there are few women – communicate readily with a few gestures: offers of bottles of tea, or sausages warmed on the backplate of boilers, or chops grilled on polished shovels in blazing fireboxes. It is the locomotives themselves that do the talking. Their language is rich, composed of a vocabulary of pulsating exhausts, singing injectors, an insistence of pistons, the chatter of connecting rods, the hum of blower valves, the urgent hiss of safety valves, shrieks of whistles, a backbeat of air brake compressors. This language has been spoken and understood for 200 years. Whatever the economic arguments for and against the steam locomotive, this compelling, creedless, classless global language brings together people from diverse and even opposed backgrounds.

In Amman, reporting for *The Guardian*, a week after the destruction of the World Trade Centre, I was stopped in my tracks by a steam whistle. It led me, unerringly, to Amman station, where a united nations of steam locomotives – German, British, Japanese – were being serviced or restored.

Amman is the headquarters of the Trans-Jordan Railway, the one that Lawrence of Arabia sabotaged to frustrate German and Turkish supply lines. Here, I enjoyed cups of sweet mint tea with the railway's chief engineer in a room adorned with models of locomotives under gently insistent ceiling fans.

We talked of locomotives, of Lawrence, and of a grand plan to extend the railway across the Jordanian and Iraqi deserts to Baghdad.

This discussion was poignant then: a westerner in an Arab country in the wake of the September 11 attack discussing local plans for trade with Iraq some 18 months before this sad country, invented by the British two years before Gresley's *Flying Scotsman* took to the rails, was invaded a second time in a dozen years, its people bombed, its infrastructure blitzed. It seems plain sad now.

I did, though, get to ride through the desert towards Ma'an on a fine, glossy black 1950s Henschel 2-8-2, with the crew offering lessons in local politics as well as in how to repair an ill-tempered brake-compressor.

Steam men are rarely dumb. I don't think they can be: a steam locomotive needs constant attention, its crews practising a craft rather than pressing buttons and twisting knobs. In France, engine drivers were called "*mécaniciens*", and in the US, "engineers". As with the drivers I have worked or ridden with in China, Poland, Cuba, India, Pakistan, Vietnam, Mozambique and England, they were able to make running repairs to their mounts.

The first steam locomotive I drove, when very young, was Ford No 8, a green Peckett industrial 0-6-0 saddle tank at Dagenham Docks beside the Thames. A tin box had to be found for me so I could stand high enough to see out of the cab. Blower valve off, reversing lever to full gear, a toot on the whistle and then that magical easing of the regulator ... this was much more fun than school, a language that, once learned, demands practice whenever and wherever it is still spoken, on high days when enthusiasts' specials run, and in the distant junctions of the world.

TREVITHICK'S COALBROOKDALE LOCOMOTIVE (1803)

↑ Richard Trevithick (1771–1833), a Cornish engineer, designed and built the world's first successful steam locomotive. King George III was on the throne; Napoleon had yet to crown himself emperor. This was the Pennydarren locomotive of 1804. It won Samuel Homfray, owner of the Pennydarren Ironworks, south Wales, a handsome £500 bet when it hauled 10 tons of pig iron and 70 men the length of the Merthyr tramway on February 21, 1804. The 9.5-mile journey took four hours, with top speeds of 5mph and frequent stops to remove obstacles and prune overhanging trees. The driver – Trevithick – walked alongside the machine to control it. The locomotive, however, proved too

heavy for the iron track. Nevertheless, Trevithick had proved his point: the steam engine could be turned into a useful locomotive. His first design, almost identical to the Pennydarren locomotive, was this engine for the Coalbrookdale company in Shropshire. It was probably built in 1803 but, as far as we know, never ran. Trevithick built another locomotive in 1805 for Wylam Colliery, Northumberland, again too heavy, and *Catch Me Who Can*, which ran around in 12mph circles as a diversion and education for Londoners, on the site of the future Euston station.

→ *Rocket* is probably the most famous of all railway locomotives, steam or otherwise. It was designed by George Stephenson (1779–1843), a Northumbrian engineer, who watched Trevithick build his Wylam Colliery locomotive. Stephenson worked for the colliery, too, which is how he began designing his own locomotives. *Rocket*, however, was very different from those early colliery and tramway locomotives. She was designed to run fast at the head of passenger trains on the Liverpool & Manchester Railway, opened in 1830. Boasting a multi-tube boiler, *Rocket* ran confidently at 30mph and more at the Rainhill Trials of 1829, when the design of locomotives for the L&M was decided. She was not the

fastest locomotive tested, but she was economical and, above all, reliable. She was painted a festive canary yellow. At the gala opening of the L&M, she ran over and mortally wounded George Huskisson, MP for Liverpool. *Rocket* was sold by the L&M in 1837. Here she is, rebuilt with lowered cylinders, a new smokebox, modified wheels, black paintwork and other alterations, in 1862. She is preserved in this condition at the Science Museum, London, while a replica of how she was in 1830 steams from the National Railway Museum, York.

↖ *Wylam Dilly* (1814), sister locomotive to *Puffing Billy*, looking a little worse for wear. Early locomotive engineers were not overly concerned about how their engines appeared. In design terms, these locomotives were functional, their form following function. Since they worked in collieries, well away from gentlefolk, looks hardly mattered. It was only with the coming of the Liverpool & Manchester Railway in 1830 that appearance needed to be taken seriously. Instead of a simple iron tube, a chimney might be based on the design of a fluted Roman column, while splashers over driving wheels might take their cue from Gothic tracery. It took some while for the aesthetic of the steam locomotive to mature.

← *Puffing Billy*, a two-cylinder 0-4-0, was built in 1813 by William Hedley to work at Wylam Colliery like the pioneering locomotives of Trevithick and Stephenson. As an advance on Trevithick's, she carried her own fuel, while driver and fireman rode aboard her. *Puffing Billy* LOOKS LIKE a stationary steam engine mounted on wheels. Although clumsy in appearance, she would have enjoyed a smoother ride than the Pennydarren locomotive, with her two vertical cylinders providing an even push as she chugged along at 8mph. This photograph was taken in 1862, proving that *Puffing Billy*, preserved in the Science Museum, London, had a long and useful life. The locomotive's tall chimney appears to be modelled on the manager's stove-pipe hat, or is it the other way around?

↑ Here is a replica of the first French steam locomotive, designed and built by the engineer Marc Seguin (1786–1875) in 1829. Significantly, Seguin had patented his multi-tube boiler two years earlier. The design was seized on eagerly by George Stephenson who placed a multi-tube boiler on the frames of *The Rocket*, which not only won the Rainhill Trials of 1829, but went on to become the mechanical blueprint for nearly every successful steam locomotive built over the following 175 years. From this very first design, French locomotive engineering proved, at its best, to be scientific, rigorous and much concerned with thermal efficiency.

↑ Didcot station, May 20, 1892. Great Western Rover class 4-2-2 *Bulkeley* takes on water at the head of the last London-bound broad-gauge mail train from Plymouth. This is an historic moment, and the crew knows it. Brunel's seven-foot, quarter-inch tracks were out of step with the rest of Britain's railways, which had adopted a standard gauge of four feet, eight-and-a-half inches. In 1892, the broad-gauge gave way to standard-gauge, making these imperious locomotives, designed originally by Daniel Gooch, redundant. Developed from 1847, Gooch 4-2-2s were masters of every task for nearly half a century. They were fast – 80mph – popular and reliable.

↗ Promontory, Utah, May 10, 1869. The final gold rivet has been driven into the track, completing the transcontinental railroad between the east and west coasts of the United States. General Ulysses S Grant, US President, did the honours. Here engineers and big-wigs celebrate with wine and champagne. The project was a collaboration between the Union Pacific, fielding 10,000 workers from Omaha beginning in December 1865, and the Central Pacific, with 12,000 workers starting out from Sacramento in January 1863. It inspired the transcontinental railways of Canada, and the Trans-Siberian route across Russia. *Jupiter*, the classic American type 4-4-0 on the left, survives.

→ To "*prendre le Crampton*" in France meant to catch an express train. The phrase was used long after long-legged Cramptons had disappeared. Thomas Crampton's locomotives were distinguished by low-slung boilers and huge single driving wheels mounted well back on their frames. From their inception on the LNWR, England, in 1847, they were fast – 120km/h – and have been neatly described as Napoleon III's TGVs. This example, No. 80, is one of twelve 4-2-0s built in Lille for the Paris-Strasbourg Railway in 1852. First withdrawn in 1914, she was restored in 1946 and is now in the French Railway Museum, Mulhouse.

Overleaf →→ A lovely study of Brunel's broad-gauge Great Western Railway and of the fine Gooch "singles" that served it for more than half a century with little need for change. *Timor* sweeps around the seafront at Dawlish, south Devon, near the end of the long run from Paddington to Plymouth c.1890. This photograph shows how well the railways were able to blend in with, and even enhance, their surroundings. There is a delightful symmetry between the steam locomotive with its copper-capped chimney and the tall, pointed tower of the parish church, and between the nave of the church and the boiler of the locomotive. William Dean improved these early Victorian machines up until the end of their long reign; they were always kept in tip-top condition.

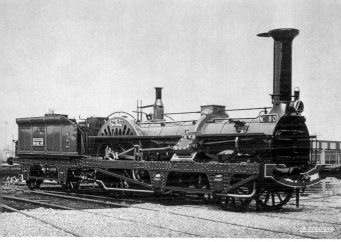

← Adelaide, 1937. This is South Australia's centenary parade. Under the bunting and along past the cheering crowd goes a replica of the first steam locomotive to run in the state. The actual engine was an outside cylinder 2-4-0T built in 1855 by William Fairbairn of Manchester for the opening of the Adelaide to Port Adelaide line the following year. This was one of three such locomotives. No 1 was converted into a tender locomotive in 1869 and scrapped by 1874. Only two sets of driving wheels from these historic locomotives survive in the National Railway Museum, Port Adelaide. The British exported locomotives around the globe.

↑ Beyer-Peacock locomotives were exported around the world, notably to Australia, from the company's works in Manchester; they were real empire builders. Here, a Beyer-Peacock, 4-4-0 tank, No. 41 of the Metropolitan Railway, built in 1864, enjoys a quiet moment on the Brill branch in the early 1930s. The barely used stations on this former Buckinghamshire tramway would have seemed like remote outposts in the Northern Territories to Londoners more familiar with electric trains to Baker Street and the City. This locomotive had once worked the world's first underground line, between Paddington and Farringdon. She was retired in 1935.

↓↓ Postcards of British trains were popular in Edwardian England. They had every right to be proud of trains like this, *The Flying Scotsman* on its 393-mile run to Edinburgh Waverley at Hadley Wood, north London, in 1906. The locomotive is one of Henry Ivatt's big Atlantics (as opposed to his small Atlantics of 1899) for the Great Northern Railway (1902). Characterised by their beefy boilers, broad fireboxes and easy steaming, these highly competent and fast machines were entrusted with the running of high-speed Pullman trains from Leeds to King's Cross in the late 1930s. They would happily run at more than 90mph and keep 60mph schedules. They gave way to Nigel Gresley's Pacifics as the weight of trains like *The Flying Scotsman* exceeded 500 tons.

↓ Supremely elegant Edwardian English locomotive design: a brand new Great Central Railway Atlantic 192, in 1906, in workshop grey. John Robinson designed her. He believed an engine's chimney should be like a gentleman's hat. These shapely 4-4-2s were fondly known as "Jersey Lillys" after Lilly Langtry, an actress and favourite squeeze of King Edward VII. Robinson's Atlantics were not just good looking; they were surprisingly fast and free steaming, too, enabling the Great Central to run its refined expresses between Sheffield, Nottingham, Leicester and Marylebone to very tight, point-to-point timings. A few of these joyous locomotives, by then painted a joyless black, survived to be nationalised in 1948, but they were from a very different era, the Golden Age of Britain's steam railways.

→ One of the world's most famous trains, *The Flying Scotsman*, leaves King's Cross on its first non-stop run to Edinburgh on May 1, 1928 behind one of the world's most famous locomotives, LNER A1 Pacific 4472 *Scotsman*. *Flying Scotsman* was built in 1923, one of the first of Nigel Gresley's fleet and powerful, three-cylinder Pacifics. These locomotives revolutionised long-distance train travel in Britain between the two world wars. The A1s were inspired by the K-4 Pacifics of the Pennsylvania Railroad. A1s seemed impossibly big and modern when first seen by the travelling public in the last days of the Great Northern Railway in 1922. *Flying Scotsman* was withdrawn, as a more efficient A3, in 1963, and has been preserved in running order ever since.

THE "FLYING SCOTSMAN" PASSING HADLEY WOODS.

↑ Without slipping, Great Western four-cylinder 4-6-0 *Pendennis Castle* (1923) pulls confidently away from King's Cross with an LNER express on April 22, 1925. *P tle* had been displayed alongside *Flying Scotsman* at the British Empire Exhibition, Wembley, 1924–5. The Great Western claimed the much smaller locomotive was the most powerful in Britain. Gresley rose to the challenge. The two were pitted against one another on tests in 1925. Gresley had to eat humble pie. Charles Collett's sure-footed 79-ton 4-6-0, despite its rather old-fashioned looks, was a superb steamer. It was fast, powerful and famously easy on coal and water. Gresley went back to the drawing board and, in 1927,

revealed his A3 "Super Pacifics", which drew on Great Western as well as the latest French practice.

↗ The one problem with the P2s was their length. Here, *Cock o' the North* is turned, with a bit of effort, at King's Cross in 1934. Up in Scotland, they were said to put undue strain on tight curves. Whatever the truth, they were rebuilt as conventional Pacifics by Edward Thompson, Gresley's successor as chief mechanical engineer of the LNER. It was often said that Thompson, who raged against the hidden complexities of Gresley's thoroughbreds, was jealous of the magnificent P2s. This may or may not be true, but it was a sad loss when these 2-8-2s re-emerged, like shorn sheep, from Doncaster Works. Although fleet of foot, they were a shadow of their former selves and were the first LNER Pacifics to be sent for scrap.

→ Andre Chapelon (1892–1978) designed the most efficient steam locomotives of his day; few have been more efficient since. Complex, beautifully engineered machines, these included several classes of Pacifics – 231 in French coding – either rebuilt from earlier designs, or else brand new for the nationalized SNCF and built up until 1939. These fleet, powerful and remarkably quiet machines could produce up to 3,400ihp, with 2,700dhp continuously available to pull heavy express passenger trains. Here, in 1967, a K-class Pacific, rebuilt from a PLM original, races past kilometre post 231 at Etaples at the head of a train from Paris Gare du Nord to Calais Maritime.

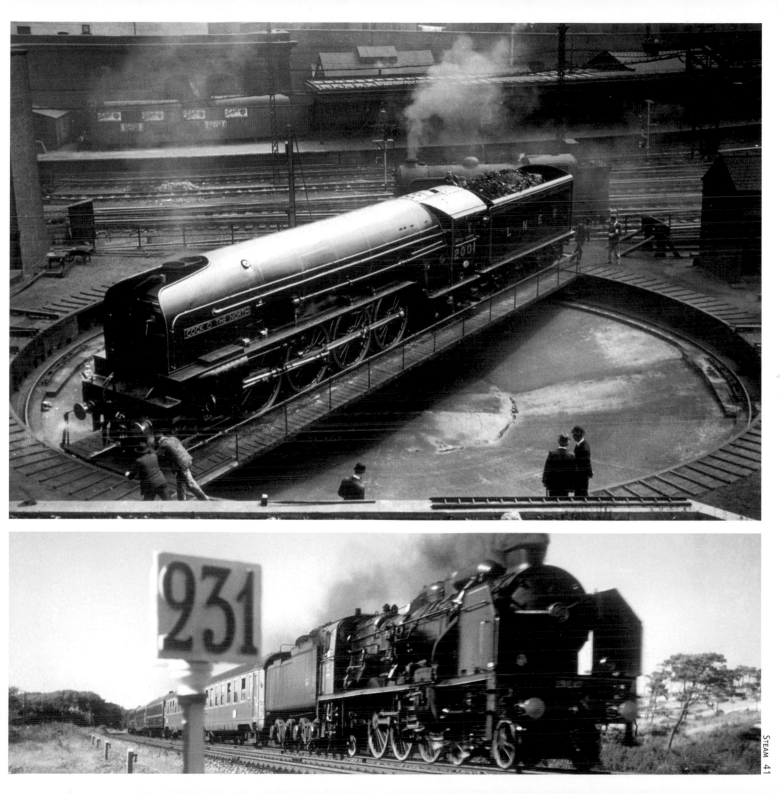

The press run of the LMS's glorious *Coronation Scot* express in June 1937 was a sensation. William Stanier's brand new four-cylinder Princess Coronation Pacific, 6220 Coronation, romped away from Euston under easy steam, before making an attempt on the world speed record on the last few downhill miles to Crewe. Still accelerating, she reached 112.5mph (114mph according to the LMS), before braking furiously for the station. Crockery broke and glasses flew in the dining car, yet the magnificent blue-and-white striped streamliner had stolen a headline march on the LNER, its rival railway to Scotland. On the way back, Coronation needed just 119 minutes to cover the 158 miles to Euston at an unprecedented average speed of 79.7mph. The journalists here at Euston seem justifiably impressed.

The *Coronation Scot* in regular service, climbing the 1-in-70 gradient of Camden Bank as it departs Euston on December 19, 1938. The 401-mile journey to Glasgow took six hours and 30 minutes, at an average speed of a little over 60mph, with a stop to change crews at Carlisle. Many commentators were disappointed with this timing, since not only was the LNER running the 393 miles up the east coast to Edinburgh in an even six hours, but the 3,300ihp Coronation Pacifics were kept on a tight rein throughout the journey. But the streamliner needed to keep to time day-in, day-out; it had to thread its way through the path of slower passenger and goods trains, a multitude of speed restrictions and permanent way works.

Now then, young ladies, who's first to polish me old oil lamp? It's June 1937, and time for a publicity shot of the brand new *Coronation Scot* streamliner at Euston station. The oil-powered headlamps have been given Art Deco wings in keeping with the locomotive's cinematic styling. This was a time when engine crews were folk heroes, their faces appearing in the newspapers along with those of managers, pretty girls and stars of screen and wireless. Largely designed by T F Coleman, while his boss, William Stanier, was away on government railway work in India, the Princess Coronation Pacifics were the equal best British express passenger locomotives. Their streamline casing was removed after the Second World War. They were withdrawn from regular service in 1964.

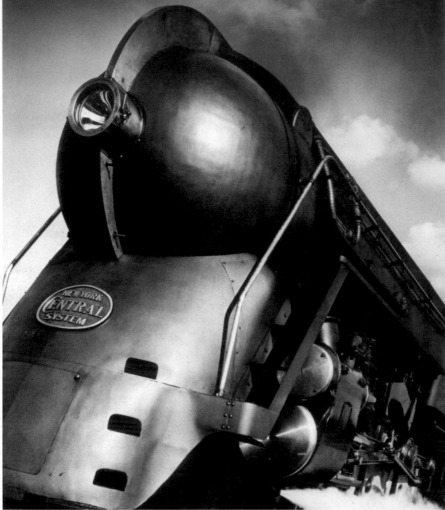

↑ A truly iconic image of one of the 10 J3-a streamlined Hudsons engineered by Paul Kiefer and styled by Henry Dreyfuss for the New York Central's 1938 20th Century Limited. Beginning on June 15, 1938, this illustrious train was scheduled from Grand Central station, New York, to La Salle Street, Chicago, in 16 hours overnight at an average speed of very nearly 60mph. Boxy T-series electric locomotives, built in the 1920s, took the train upstate from smokeless New York city, the first 33 miles to Harmon in 46 minutes, handing over to a sequence of J3-as for the rest of the run. The 20th Century Limited cruised at 85mph – there was a speedo in the observation car for passengers to check – but if necessary these impressive 4,700ihp, two-cylindered 4-6-4s could run very much faster. When they went on display to an impressed public at Grand Central on June 13 and 14, 1938, the great locomotives had to be towed, fireless, from Harmon by decidedly unglamorous T2-a electrics. Still, 65,000 NewYorkers turned out to review the new streamliners, while, between them, Kiefer and Dreyfuss had projected the image of the steam express into the future even though General Motors was on the march.

↑ J3-a 5453, Chicago, 1938. The Hudson is painted silver grey, with polished cylinder heads and other details. Note the Scullin disc wheels, much stronger than spokes, yet rare at the time. The locomotive's finish was designed to gleam as the sun set over the Hudson River while the 20th Century Limited curved away from Harmon, and passengers prepared for dinner. The streamlined locomotives were used extensively in NYC publicity, although it is interesting to note how new GM diesels shown in calendars and timetable brochures from 1946 gradually nosed ahead of the NYC's Hudsons by 1948. This was the year they took charge of the 20th Century, and in more senses than one. Kiefer made one last great attempt at beating the encroaching diesels with his S-1 Niagara class 4-8-4s of 1945. Occasionally one of these titans took charge of the 20th Century, making Dreyfuss's great train look Lilliputian. As for Dreyfuss, a giant among industrial designers, the 20th Century Limited was one of his few railroad commissions. His prodigious and brilliant career had begun in 1929, ending with his suicide, jointly with his cancer-stricken wife, in 1972, by which time his peerless train was a folk memory.

↖ King's Cross, 1963: Gresley A4 Pacific *Mallard*, ass BR 60022, at the end of her 25-year main line career, and still very much an object of admiration. *Mallard* is credited with being the world's fastest steam locomotive. On July 3, 1938, she apparently reached 126mph (202km/h), with driver Duddington and fireman Bray at the controls, down Stoke Bank between Grantham and Peterborough at the head of a seven-coach test train. *Mallard's* top speed may "only" have been 124.5/125mph, but for her fans, British had to be best. Whatever the truth, A4s were speedy; on the 1935 press run of the Silver Jubilee streamliner, 2509 *Silver Link* averaged 100mph for 43 miles on end, topping 112.5mph twice.

← Journalists at the American Locomotive Works, Schenectady, New York, crowd around the first of the streamlined, two-cylinder Atlantics custom-designed for the Milwaukee's Hiawatha express, April 30, 1935. This legendary train, which boasted the fastest ever steam schedule (81.6mph), was expected to run at 100mph or more whenever necessary to maintain time over a competitive route. It is possible that these 3,300ihp 4-4-2s may have reached 120mph. What we know for certain is that they ran hard and fast nearly every day of their brief, if spectacular, lives. We also know that the 4,700ihp Hudsons that came to share the running of the Hiawatha with them were equally fast; one averaged 100mph for 62

miles with a 1,000-ton train. No British Pacific could get anywhere close.

↑ Streamlined DR 4-6-4 05 002 is generally considered to be the fastest all-round steam locomotive. Built by Borsig in 1935 under the direction of Rudolf Wagner, the 3,400ihp locomotive was timed, accurately, at 124.5mph (201km/h), a speed she maintained rather than nudged. She exceeded 110mph several times. In 1936, British journalists and railway experts, including William Stanier of the LMS and Cecil J Allen, the meticulous recorder of train speeds, rode behind her from Berlin to Hamburg; 05 002 glided at 118mph with ease. Here she is, a magnificent example of engineering skill and scientific research, at Hamburg in 1936. She survived the war, but was rebuilt

without her red streamlined casing. She was broken up in 1960. Her sister engine, 05 001, is preserved.

↓ What were the most powerful steam locomotives? There are several contenders, but among the most consistent high-powered performers were the last of the Union Pacific's articulated Mallets. Charged with hauling immense freight trains across the United States during the Second World War, these needed to be fast as well as muscular. Twenty-five 541-ton Big Boy 4-8-8-4s were built in 1941–2 for this essential work; 4011 is the train engine of this double-headed freight train pounding up Sherman Hill, between Laramie and Cheyenne, Wyoming. Big Boys could develop over 6,500dhp, haul 8,000-ton freight trains, and run at 80mph; they were strong, but not muscle bound. They worked hard through

the 1950s, much loved by those who crewed and managed them. The leading engine is 3999, a Challenger 4-6-6-4, one of a class of 105 built from 1936. These giants, which could run at 70–80mph, were often used on passenger trains on steeply graded lines. One has been retained by the Union Pacific for commemorative and enthusiasts' specials. Both classes of engines were meticulously groomed. Try to imagine the basso profundo music these two giants are making as they tackle this notoriously demanding grade with something like 12,000dhp between them to pull this train.

→ This photograph is, delightfully, captioned "The British royal family's train passes beneath Mount Stephen, in the Rocky Mountains, on a state visit to Canada, 1939." It would have been odd, not to say plain eccentric, of King George VI and Queen Elizabeth to have chosen a freight train when they might have ridden by Pullman. This train, climbing the Rockies, is, in fact, an unidentified Canadian Pacific freight locomotive working a heavy livestock train hard up a long incline with Mt Stephen dominating the backdrop. The locomotive is possibly a P-2-e 2-8-2, one of many powerful 2-8-2s built for the Canadian Pacific from the mid-1920s until 1944. These boasted vast 23 x 32-inch

cylinders, a boiler pressure of 275psi and 63-inch driving wheels, and lasted until the end of steam on the Canadian Pacific at the beginning of the 1960s. They were masters of their job. The royal train would have been pulled by one of the Royal Hudsons. These were magnificent, semi-streamlined 4-8-4s built from 1937, the year King George VI was crowned. Painted black, silver and deep re d, these made a splendid and powerful sight crossing the great Canadian landscape. This line across the Rockies was their stamping ground, too.

↓ When, after independence, the Indian Railways needed a new broad-gauge (5ft 3in) passenger workhorse, their engineers took their cue from the XP Pacifics of the Great India Peninsula Railway. These had been developed in the late 1930s after a study tour of Indian locomotives made by, among others, William Stanier, chief mechanical engineer of the LMS. The result was the WP 4-6-2, a class of 755 locomotives built at home and abroad from 1947 until 1967. Despite their semi-streamlined appearance, and often ornate decoration, these rugged and straightforward two-cylinder Pacifics were designed specifically to burn low-calorie, high-ash Indian coal, which is why they always appeared to be so smoky. The result was a locomotive that was cheap to run and maintain, and able to slog at 55mph over long distances with heavy trains and without fuss. I was lucky enough to ride the footplate of one of these handsome locomotives from Old Delhi shortly before they disappeared from service in the late 1980s. We had four fireman (I was one), rumbled along at a steady 60mph and were covered in soot long before we arrived in Chandigarh. I'd forgotten that I had a business meeting and needed to look smart.

→ In distant Moscow, Leonid Brezhnev is in the Kremlin as the old Communist order declines into a new era of repression and general glumness. Here, in snowy Skovorodino in the depths of Siberia, is something altogether more liberating and glamorous: the majestic sight of a Soviet Railways two-cylinder P-36 4-8-4 at the head of the Rossiya. The year is 1970, and this handsome locomotive — the first appeared in 1953 — is looking as good as new. Designed for Trans-Siberian and Leningrad-Moscow expresses, such as the prestigious Red Arrow, the P-36 was the last express passenger type developed in the USSR. They were a blend of the best Russian, German and American elements, free-steaming, fast, powerful, economical, reliable and easy to maintain. They developed 3,500ihp, were timed at 106mph although they rarely exceeded 75mph in daily service (this was quite unnecessary in Russia, where consistency and time-keeping mattered far more than speed) and always seemed to look as well turned out as 0250 pictured here. Taking photographs of trains in the former Soviet Union was a crime; you needed to get up on freezing, sunny mornings, before anyone in their right (or left) mind would be out of their bunk to notice.

← The *Golden Arrow* Pullman leaves Victoria station, London, at 11a.m. on its 90-minute run to Dover Western Docks in 1961. Here it will meet the British Railway's steamship *Invicta*. Across the Channel, passengers will rendezvous with the *Fleche d'Or* for the journey on to Paris. This glamorous train ran from 1929 to 1972, with steam power giving way to electric in 1961. The handsome locomotive is West Country Pacific 34100 Appledore, one of 110 lightweight, three-cylinder, 86-ton 4-6-2s designed by Oliver Bulleid (1882–1970) for the Southern Railway; Bulleid was much influenced by the designs of the great French engineer, André Chapelon (1892–1978). Appledore, originally streamlined, was built in 1949, rebuilt in 1960 by British Railways by R Jarvis of Brighton Works, and withdrawn in 1967. Fast, powerful, efficient, Appledore was a good ambassador for Britain's nationalised railways in their steam heyday. The train looks splendid: the engine is painted Brunswick green, the Pullman cars, some way behind, in chocolate and cream.

↓ The scene is Calais Maritime. Passengers are transferring from the *Canterbury*, or *Invicta*, ferry boat to the *Fleche d'Or*. A weighty and beautifully appointed train, it will make its dash to Paris Gare du Nord behind this smooth-running and near silent Chapelon Nord 231E, 101-ton, four-cylinder compound Pacific. Built from 1934, the 231E was a development of an existing P & O Railway design for Compagnie du Nord. When fully extended, these locomotives could reach 110mph and sustain a prodigious power output of 2,700dbhp on the road. A maximum of 3,400ihp was developed at the SNCF's Vitry-sur-Seine test plant. This, however, paled into insignificance when compared to the 4,000ihp produced by Chapelon's 240P class four-cylinder compound, 111-ton 4-8-0, and 5300ihp for his solitary 1946 242A1 three-cylinder compound 4-8-4. Chapelon's were the world's most efficient steam locomotives; crews and passengers alike loved them. They ran from Calais to Paris until 1971.

← In the last days of regular British Railways' main line steam, Colin T Gifford, a distinguished photographer, travelled through the declining industrial towns of Lancashire to record their passing. The brilliance of his sombre pictures lies in his recording of the landscapes, places and people these ill-kempt survivors served, as well as the locomotives themselves. The best of his photographs have a poignancy that brings one close to tears; not as a lament for passing steam, but for people who worked so hard for so little, and were offered back the worst of everything. This Lancashire town, Wigan, looks cold and bleak one winter's morning in early 1968 as a Stanier 8F 2-8-0 climbs past rows of harsh red brick terraces with a heavy, fitted freight.

↑ Rain, steam and mud. A Colin T Gifford study of a Stanier Class 5 4-6-0 powering an unfitted coal train over a sooty brick viaduct and past semaphore signals in Wigan, 1968. Imagine yourself as the chap in the cloth cap tramping down this dank path on an overcast day spitting with rain. Fine if you happen to be a keen-eyed photographer, or railway enthusiast, but for anyone else? Much of the world of the steam locomotive revolved around coal, soot, oil, water, leaks and general grime. But there was no reason for the steam world to be so grubby. In Britain, the rise of consumerism and autophilia coincided with a general contempt for the railways. By 1997, a cynical government had flogged the lot off.

Overleaf →→ Photographer Colin Garratt has devoted years of his life to travelling the world in search of steam. This is one of his rewards. In February 2003, a pair of well-kept Chinese Railways QJ 2-10-2s thunder across a concrete bridge through the Jinpeng Pass, Inner Mongolia. This dramatic line, running through bravura and largely uninhabited landscapes, opened in 1996. Its job, like that of these 3,500ihp QJs, is to bring raw materials down to the country's developing cities. Steam locomotives were chosen for the line because, at heart, they are simple, rugged machines that are cheap to build and can be repaired with a spanner, a hammer and a bit of muscle. These are useful assets in a landscape like this.

58

DIESEL + ELECTRIC

There are diesel engines, electric trains and diesel-electric locomotives. The first were an invention of Rudolph Diesel, a German engineer, in 1897. The second, powered by batteries, were developed in the United States in model form as early as 1837, by Thomas Davenport, and, by Robert Davidson for real, in England, five years later. The first electric train to pick up current as it ran was by Siemens and Halske in Germany, 1879 (p60). But it was the third of these – the diesel-electric – that challenged, and then ousted, steam locomotives worldwide.

Electric trains are undeniably fast, clean and efficient. Their one problem is that electric railways are expensive to build and demand scrupulous maintenance. In remote, inhospitable and poor parts of the world, money may be too tight, while power supplies, where they exist, may be too erratic. Although fundamentally reliable, electric trains require more know-how to run and repair than steam or diesel locomotives. With honourable exceptions, such as Cuba's vintage Hershey overhead electric system that still stretches from Mendoza to Havana, the electric train is predominant in the world's most advanced economies, and spectacularly so in France and Japan.

Enter the all-conquering diesel-electric. The first successful diesel locomotive, built in Switzerland by Sulzer, ran as early as 1912, while the Deutsche Reichsbahn's lightweight Fliegende Hamburger was thrumming along at 160km/h between Hamburg and Berlin from 1932. The diesel-electrics that were to change the face, and sound, of world railways emerged from the EMD division of General Motors in the US from 1937. What GM offered was robust, low-revving diesel engines powering General Electric traction motors that, in turn, powered the axles of the new, all-enclosed locomotives.

This was not an ideal way to burn fuel, but in terms of thermal efficiency, diesel-electrics were way in advance of steam locomotives. The more important thing, though, is that these big diesels could start at the turn of a key. They could be coupled in series to meet power demands with a single crew in charge. They were superficially clean - their exhausts were lethal – reliable, and came with GM guarantees and back-up service.

Other forms of diesel locomotives have been tried; the much lighter diesel-hydraulics popular on the Deutsche Bundesbahn and British Railway's Western Region in the 1950s and 1960s, and diesel-mechanicals, many of them DMUs (diesel multiple units) requiring the driver to change gear as the train accelerated. None, though, was as successful as the all-purpose diesel-electric.

I am afraid to say that I do not have a favourite diesel locomotive. I know the early US Alco and GM diesel-electrics have their fans. I can understand the appeal of the high-revving and complex 3,300hp English Electric Deltics (BR class 55) that once ran from King's Cross to Edinburgh. For me, though, diesels were always an aberration. Railways might have gone from steam to electric wherever possible, with the steam locomotive developed for use elsewhere.

Like many, I am impressed by, if not in love with, the latest generation of serpentine high-speed EMUs (electric multiple units) that race across much of western Europe and Japan today. I enjoy the efficiency of Swiss electric trains, and the effortless acceleration of heavy expresses in eastern Europe and Russia. I like the arcs of electricity that flash, like fireworks, from commuter trains winding in and out of London on frosty winter mornings.

And one of my favourite train journeys of all was from Milan to Rome on the Italian State Railway's flamboyant "Il Settebello" (p70). Lunch was served dressed with oil far too good for diesel engines , while the view from the forward observation car was electrifying.

↑ All aboard the world's first electric train. This is the Siemens & Halske experimental electric train running along 600 yards of track at the Berlin Trade Exhibition, 1879. The tiny, four-wheeled locomotive picked up current from a third rail set between the narrow-gauge tracks. With 3hp on tap, it pulled three park bench-style carriages with up to 26 bewhiskered and crinolined Berliners at 4mph. Experiments with battery-powered electric trains date from 1835, but this was the first train to pick up continuous electric current, and the begetter of every tram, metro train and main-line electric train ever since.

→ The Baltimore & Ohio commissioned three of these General Electric 1,500hp Bo-Bo locomotives in 1895 to pull freight trains of up to 1,800 tons through the steeply graded Howard Street tunnel beneath Baltimore harbour. This rid the tunnel of the dense exhaust of steam freight locomotives, which would carry on their work after the electrics had ferried their trains cleanly underground. The B&O was not the first US railroad to run electrics; that honour goes to the Saratoga, Mount McGregor and Lake George, New York, which electrified 12 miles of track in 1883 to the of English-born engineer Leo Daft.

↓ Electric trains arrived surprisingly early in India, the first between Bombay Victoria and Kurla in February 1925. Main line electrics like this 1-D-1 began running in the 1930s on the GIPR in the Bombay region. Electrification in the Calcutta area began in 1953-4, and the first modern 25kv AC electric services in 1957 between Burdwan and Mughalsarai, using French technology and locomotives. A big debate over whether Indian Railways should invest in diesel or electric technology in the 1960s and 1970s was finally decided by the Oil Crisis of 1973-74; electric traction finally won the day, and the leading trains of the sub-continent.

↓↓ Swiss railways made early and effective use of electric locomotives for main-line passenger services. Their ability to maintain even speeds uphill and down made them a firm favourite with operators in this mountainous country. This is a BLS (Berne Lotschberg Simplon Railway) series Be5/7 1-E-1 2,500hp electric locomotive built in 1910 for the Swiss section of services between Berne and Milan. Early electrics were no more, and no less, than powerful and plain boxes on wheels.

↓ A Canadian National Z1a 2400v DC Bo-Bo electric pulls a train of heavy clerestory stock over Wellington Street as it exits Montreal on its way to Toronto or Ottowa. The approach through a three-mile tunnel to the CN's terminus spelled the need for early electrification. Electric trains began running from Montreal to Lazard in 1914, where these boxcab General Electric locomotives gave way to steam. These veterans enjoyed a long life, running until 1995 when the vintage electric system was replaced. This was a similar system to that employed by the New York Central from Grand Central to Harmon.

→ Newcastle Quayside, 1905. The North Eastern Railway faced the same problem as the B&O: how to negotiate heavy freight trains through steep and slippery city tunnels. Two of these bright green locomotives were built by Brush Engineering, Loughborough, from imported General Electric components. They ran until 1964. The NER had intended to electrify its York to Newcastle main line in the 1920s. A 90mph, 1,800hp locomotive was built under the direction of Vincent Raven in 1922, but the plan and the locomotive were scrapped, leaving steam to reign supreme on the open road away from slippery quayside tunnels for another 40 years.

← Looking like an angry bullfrog, this is the Union Pacific's M10001 *City of Portland* diesel-electric streamliner ready to leap into action between Chicago and Portland in June 1935. The UP kicked off a spate of early lightweight, air-conditioned, aluminium diesel streamliners with the M10000 *City of Salina* in 1934. Designed to lure a car-crazy American public back on to the rails, and powered by a 1,200hp V16 Winton engine, this train was said to be capable of 120mph. It was never that quick, yet gave the impression of a new, rocket-fast era on rails. In October 1934 she ran a promotional trip across the continent from Los Angeles to New York – 3,248 miles – in a record 56 hours and 55 minutes.

Passenger traffic on US railroads had fallen by two-thirds between 1920 and 1932. During those years, diesel pioneers, notably Harold Harrison of Electro Motive Engineering, which he founded and which was later taken over by General Motors, designed and built a number of early diesel shunters and railcars. Rudolph Diesel's engine had been developed in 1897, but it was another quarter of a century before it challenged steam dominance on the main line. *City of Portland*, which helped start that trend, ran until 1939.

↑ A streamlined Bugatti "Automotrice", self-propelled railcar for the SNCF. The great French automotive engineer, Ettore Bugatti, left the design of the classic Type-57 roadster to focus on the development of these fast, lightweight railcars powered by the 12.7-litre, 8-cylinder, 200bhp engines from the massive Bugatti Royale. Built between 1933 and 1938, the one-, two- or three-car units ran on industrial petrol-alcohol fuel. The cost of this rose greatly as the 1930s progressed, and the railcars were abandoned on grounds of high running costs. Not, though, before one had, temporarily, taken the world railway speed record at 196kph [122mph] in 1934.

← December 17, 1937: a revolution in the making. This is the brand new *City of Los Angeles* diesel-electric streamliner on its way through Spring Valley, 30 miles north of New York, to a railroad exhibition in the city. Its regular route will be Chicago to Los Angeles. The striking yellow and red striped 14-car train is a quarter of a mile long; the General Motors E2 power units leading it to Manhattan are geared for a theoretical 117mph; no wonder the crowd looks shocked and awed. General Motors, with sales and marketing guns blazing, had gone into the diesel business in 1930, sounding an early death knell for the steam railway locomotive worldwide. A New York Central L2A fast freight Mohawk 4-8-2

thunders past in the opposite direction. These fine general purpose machines, dating from 1925–6, would be among the last steam locomotives to run the "Water Level Route" in 1956.

↓ A colourful line-up of ALCo PA1 and GM F7 diesel-electrics at the St Louis railroad yard, Missouri, in the mid-1960s. These two hugely successful locomotive types effectively did for steam traction across the United States. General Motors had gone into the diesel game before the Second World War, while ALCo was building massive steam freight locomotives like the Union Pacific Big Boy 4-8-8-4. It attempted to catch up, with the 2,250hp PA series, from 1946. Both GM and ALCo types have their devoted fans. The new diesels were not ultimately as fast as the latest US steam passenger locomotives, nor as powerful However, they could be coupled together in series and operated by

a single crew when brute power was needed; and they pulled away rapidly from stops and were considered to be easier to maintain than even the most efficient steam engines. Even then, it was a close-run thing between the best of the last of US steam and the slickly marketed new diesels, backed by an increasingly powerful oil lobby.

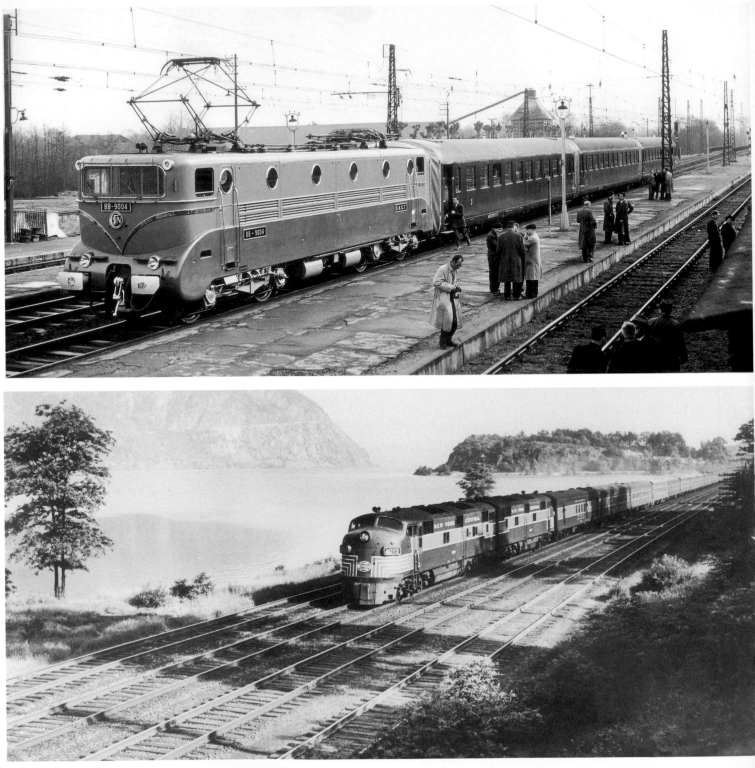

↖ France, 1955. At rest after breaking the world speed rail record, at 331km/h, between Lamothe and Morcenx south of Bordeaux on March 28, this is SNCF's BB-9004. One of two experimental 80-ton electric locomotives built in 1953, BB-9004 shared the record jointly with CC-7107, one of 58 electric passenger locomotives built between 1952 and 1959; these pointed the way to regular 200km/h running on French main lines, starting with the Mistral in 1967. In their 1955 dash, with three coaches in tow, the two locomotives buckled the track and overhead power supply, and were very nearly de-railed. BB-9004, withdrawn in 1973, is preserved at Mulhouse.

← United States, 1955. The diesel era 20th Century Limited, from New York to Chicago, bowling along the Hudson Valley. Geared for 100mph, this twin E7 diesel has 4,500hp on tap to haul the luxurious overnight express. The 42 E7s, built by General Motors (1945–49), were just one regiment in the army of bulldog-nosed E-type diesels that pushed steam aside. Their reign lasted 40 years. Cary Grant rode behind one on his fugitive ride in Hitchcock's *North by North West* (p.227). In 1957, more Americans flew than took the train, and this legendary train was to make its last run 11 years later.

↑ Great Britain, 1955. Prototype 3,300hp English-Electric Deltic departing Liverpool Lime Street on an express to London Euston. Although closely resembling a GM E7, this 106-ton diesel-electric boasts twin Napier 18-cylinder Deltic engines, adopted from the marine industry; compact, complex and free-revving, they made this the world's most powerful single-unit diesel locomotive for some years. Twenty-two 99-ton production units were built (1961–62) to replace fast A-series steam Pacifics on British Railways' East Coast main line. Named after regiments and racehorses, these popular diesels, with their distinctive, high-pitched machine-gun exhausts, were timed at up to 113mph.

↑ Faversham, Kent, England, 1959. A spectacle of statutory, short-trousered schoolboys watch as a new north Kent, third-rail electric thrums towards a level-crossing on its run from London Victoria to the coast at Ramsgate. These sturdy, prosaic 1,000hp, 90mph, four-car 4CEP units (1957–63) had just replaced a variety of much-loved steam locomotives, Schools, King Arthurs and Battle of Britains among them. What they lacked in glamour, they made up for by running day in, day out, for 45 years with a minimum of fuss. They were originally painted a deep green that blended comfortably into the Garden of England.

→ Highly styled ETR301 express: this is one of three sets of swish, green and grey electric expresses launched in 1953 (the third in 1959), for 180km/h running on the exclusive Settebello service between Milan and Rome. The crew sits up top above the observation car, with its flouncy sun blinds. Inside, individual armchairs boast fly-away headrests; fashionable murals adorn walls; bags are stored in a separate luggage car; meals are up to the standard of de luxe Italian restaurants. These exceptional trains, mobile exhibitions of 1950s Italian design, ran in regular service until 1984; one unit has been restored for special runs.

A Paris-Brussels TEE (Trans European Express) streaks along behind a CC40101 SNCF electric locomotive in 1965. Built expressly for TEE services, this class of 10 locomotives (1964–70) was designed, under the direction of Paul Arzens, to run on most European railways, Spain and Portugal excluded. As a result, these striking "broken-nosed" locomotives, the longest built for the SNCF, were ingeniously equipped to handle four different electricity supplies. For most of their lives, based at Chapelle depot, Paris, they ran the two-hour 30-minute express services to Brussels. The TGVs that replaced them in 1996 cut this journey to just one hour 20 minutes. All 10 locomotives were named – a rarity in France – and were much liked for their exclusivity, their futuristic aesthetic and their dazzling turn of speed; although nominally limited to 160km/h, two of the locomotives were timed at 230km/h. Despite their length, the locomotives weighed just 109 tons, and with up to 3,340kW to hand, these were powerful, if complex machines, requiring more time with their resident mechanics and electricians than the SNCF was used to. This lovely image, however, captures the optimistic 1950s TEE ideal of clean, fast, luxurious and, above all, modern express trains racing across a continent free of war.

TEE express *Rheingold*, 1971, on its long journey from Geneva through Germany along the Rhine Valley – Freiburg-Karlsruhe-Mannheim-Mainz-Koblenz-Bonn-Köln-Düsseldorf-Duisburg – to the Hook of Holland. The massive, egg-shaped locomotive of this handsome, colour-coded express is a DB E103.1. Developed from a class of locomotives which originally went into service in 1965, the E103.1 was mass produced by Siemens, AEG, Henschel and Krauss-Maffei, among other famous German locomotive works, for Inter City and TEE services including the Beethoven, Erasmus and Prinz Eugen, between 1970 and 1974. As powerful as it looks – 7,780kW – this teutonic, 114-ton cream and red streamliner is designed to run at 200km/h but, in 1973 and equipped with a 10,400kW motor, 103.118 reached 252.9km/h, beaten by 103.001, at 283km/h, in 1985. These charismatic locomotives were popular with crews, engineers, railway management and enthusiasts alike; and, just as a CC40101 with its Gallic nose could only be French, so the 145-strong 103.1 class was as German as a coal-scuttle helmet. The class extended its sphere of activity from 1989 with the reunification of Germany after the fall of the Berlin Wall. Many remained in front-line service in the first decade of the 21st century. The TEE *Rheingold* last ran in 1987.

↓ The streamlining of electric locomotives began with the impressive, 100mph, 216-ton GG1 class of the Pennsylvania Railroad, designed, with styling by renowned industrial designer Raymond Loewy, to run passenger services along the 226-mile New York-Philadelphia-Baltimore-Washington corridor. The 139-strong GG1 fleet (built 1934–43) hauled heavy freight trains, too. The PRR wanted to electrify further in the 1950s but new, federally subsidised national highways, airport construction programmes and the jet airliner put paid to new investment. In 1983, at the end of its life, GG1 4882 passes through Harrison, New Jersey, with an 11-coach train for New York.

↘ Perhaps the most luxurious diesel multiple units built outside the US, the five, eel-like Blue Pullman units put into service from 1960 between London and Manchester, and Birmingham and south Wales, were a vision of a future that a damp, old-fashioned British travelling public was not ready for. Up-to-the-minute and all-of-a-piece, they featured suspended floors, double-glazing, Venetian blinds, air conditioning, reclining, foam-filled First Class seats, gourmet menus and smooth, powerful brakes. Despite all this, the 90mph diesel-electrics were not a commercial success. By then painted grey, they last ran between London and Swansea in 1973.

→ Electric eel: this is an FS ETR450 Pendolino snaking its way from Rome to Milan. These technologically advanced 250km/h electric multiple units went into service in 1988, after an 18-year development programme based on a technology sold to the Italian State Railways by British Rail. Being able to tilt, these rapid trains could approach bends at considerably faster speeds than conventional express trains. In 1996, a new series, the ETR500, began running at 300km/h. These intelligent trains were the culmination of a continuous development programme by the FS that had begun with the streamlined 160km/h ETR200 series, which ran from 1936.

↑　In 1996, a 30-year old Canadian-built 2,400hp MLW Bombardier diesel-electric growls up the 110km roller-coaster track from Cusco to Aguas Calientes with a tourist train bound for Machu Picchu, the "lost" Inca city hidden in the clouds and discovered by Hiram Bingham in 1911. There are humming birds and orchids along the way. Operated by Peru Rail, these trains have since been repainted blue and yellow. The Peruvian railways are the highest in the world. If you are lucky, and have the lungs or oxygen, you can cross the top of the railway world by steam special.

↗　A fast and heavy coal train roars towards the camera at Grand Cache, Alberta, in 1999. The North American Free Trade Agreement (NAFTA) of 1994 between Canada, the United States and Mexico boosted rail freight traffic across the US-Canadian border by more than 10 per cent a year; it was predicted that soon enough this would account for half of Canadian National's business. The rugged 4,300hp SD75I diesel-electric at the head of the train is itself a product of US-Canadian collaboration; this series was built from 1996, to deal with heavier, faster freight trains, at General Motors Diesel Division, London, Ontario.

→　A pair of new New Victorian Railways diesel-electric feight locomotives towing a heavy train. Many of the railways of Australia, Canada and the United States are no longer famous for their passenger trains; in fact, many have given up running passenger trains altogether. What they do instead, today, often out of sight of most townspeople, is to transport vast amounts of goods that otherwise would be carried by trucks, at between 60 and 80mph. The vast majority are hauled by robust locomotives like these; their technology dates back 60 years, but they are rugged and reliable forms of motive power.

Overleaf →→　An immense, diesel-hauled freight train, photographed by Diana Mayfield, rolls across the blistering outback of Western Australia in 2000 on its way from Perth to Port Augusta. The promise of this railway adventure, stretching east from Kalgoorie, helped forge Australia into a federation in 1901. Construction took place through sandstorms, "blowies" and immense heat between 1912 and 1917. Scenes like this explain the appeal of the long-distance freight train not just to enthusiasts, musicians and hobos, but to anyone with a concern for the environment and common sense: think how many road trains would be needed to transport this apparently infinite load.

↑↑ Prognathous Eurostar trains basking under the glass roof of Waterloo International, designed by Nicholas Grimshaw, 1994. The Channel Tunnel service, which started that year, had been a dream dating back before Trevithick's Pennydarren locomotive turned a wheel. These complex 752-ton electric trains (1993–95), formed of 18 coaches seating 770 and two power units, pick up electricity from three power sources. With a 25kV supply, they have 12,200kW (16,600hp) on tap and, running at a maximum of 300km/h, take two hours 35 minutes from Waterloo to Paris, Gare du Nord. They cost $40,000 per passenger seat to build compared with $250,000 for rival jet aircraft. Efficiency on rails.

↑ British Rail's Inter City 125 HST turbo-charged sets, which went into regular service in 1976, proved to be the world's fastest scheduled diesel trains. Capable of cruising at 125mph, one unit was timed at 143mph. Each of the twin 2,250hp power cars, styled by Kenneth Grange, weighed just 70 tons; although noisy and smoky, they could move and, in 2004, were still a mainstay of non-electrified main-line, and cross-country, British express services. A testament to the research and development skills of British Rail – a national railway network stupidly privatised in 1997 – several HSTs have clocked up five million miles in service.

↗↗ Before the triumph of the latest generation of 250–300km/h electric trains, experiments with alternative forms of motive power were conducted worldwide, and notably in the guise of these 2,800hp, tilting gas-turbine Turbotrains developed by the United Aircraft Corporation for Amtrak and Canadian National. Although tested at 170mph, and running up to 120mph in daily service between New York and Boston, and Montreal and Toronto, these exciting, dog-nosed all-aluminium speedsters were unreliable on services requiring frequent stops. The American sets, just seven years old, were withdrawn in 1975; CN Turbotrains, like this one, lasted a few years longer.

↑ A 1969, corrugated aluminium, Budd-built Metroliner hustles through Harrison, New Jersey, on one of its last runs from Washington to New York in 1980. These electric multiple units were designed to run at up to 160mph on Penn Central services along the north-east coast corridor. Taken over by Amtrak in 1971, these original Metroliners soon burned themselves out and were replaced by electric locomotive-hauled stock. Although one blunt-nosed Metroliner did reach 164mph – remarkable, given its barn-like aerodynamic – they normally ran at no more than 100mph. They were important for clawing inter-city air passengers back on to American rails.

→ These startling orange, 260km/h TGV Sud-Est electrics began racing from Paris to Lyons in 1981. The SNCF's TGV (*train à grande vitesse*) concept was revolutionary: a comprehensive system of tracks, signalling and trains making rail services more than competitive with domestic airliners. In 1990, a TGV Atlantique reached 515km/h, a world record for a conventional train. To cope with demand, double-deck TGV Duplex trains began running between Lyons and Paris in 1996. TGV Nords average 254.5km/h every day between Lille Europe and Paris Roissy-CDG. TGV has been the state railway's "*grand projet*", changing the image of rail travel worldwide.

14

← If a duck-billed platypus was ever transformed into a train.... One of the extraordinary 285km/h, shovel-nosed 700-series Shinkansen bullet trains of the Japanese Railways. From a standing start here at Hakata station, this 13,200kW, 16-car train will average 2 42.5km/h to Shin-Osaka. The 700-series (1997–2004) replaced earlier Shinkansen units dating back to the inauguration of the first "new trunk line" ("Shinkansen") high-speed Tokyo to Shin-Osaka service in October 1964. The Shinkansen network was planned from 1956. The speed and efficiency of these trains, running at three-minute intervals and almost never late, was a challenge to railways in the West.

↓ Tokyo, 2003: 100-series (left) and 300-series (right) Shinkansen trains. The bullet-nosed 220km/h, 16-car 100-series, which went into service in 1985, made its final run in September 2003 between Shin-Osaka and Hakata. One of its replacements was the track-hugging, 270km/h 300-series, which entered service in 1992. Travel on Shinkansen is immensely more civilised than it was 40 years ago, with 70 per cent of coaches on board these "super dream trains" now smoke-free. Seats are turned to face the direction of travel. Travelling by Shinkansen offers the one great advantage of flying — speed — without the anxiety, tedium and security mania of airports.

↓ The 14.35 Nozomi 22 slips away from Hakata. This rapier-like train is a 300km/h 500-series Shinkansen, which went into service in 1997. Future Shinkansen designs include trains that can tilt and top 350km/h, while more high-speed lines are planned throughout Japan. It was recognised nearly 50 years ago that the car, although a desirable possession, was not a realistic way to get about quickly on the crowded roads of Japan. The Shinkansen project encouraged railways in France — and eventually Italy, Germany, Britain and Spain — to increase speeds dramatically, and economically, to leave even the fastest car in the new trains' wake.

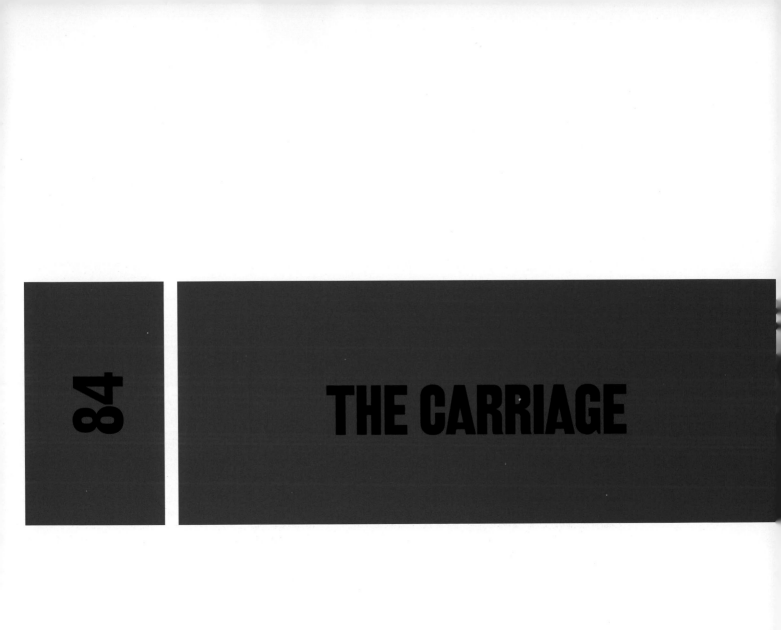

84

THE CARRIAGE

Travelling together by train as children, we learned to cough violently and otherwise act up to deter strangers from entering the compartment of our carriage. Occasionally, but not always, this tactic paid off. Later, I learned from Vivien Stanshall, the eccentric front man of the Bonzo Dog Band, that the best way to discourage other passengers from entering your compartment was to smile alluringly while beckoning them towards you with a long, slow and suggestive movement of finger or hand. This was guaranteed to work...ninety-nine times out of a hundred; if it failed, you were in trouble.

Travelling through the rest of the world taught me that it is perhaps only the English who prefer to travel alone in this way. One of life's small pleasures is to sit alone in a compartment, with an unread open book, watching fresh or familiar landscapes rush past. I have no objection to ticket inspectors, restaurant car or trolley attendants breaking my reveries, yet I still find myself bridling inwardly when someone else slides open the door and settles into the seat opposite.

Today, of course, there is a real fear that they will start eating, mouth wide open, as soon as sitting down, or playing wilfully intrusive personal stereos or making loud, interminable mobile phone calls; or all three at once. Throughout continental Europe, no one seems to mind — and much less in India, Russia, China or the length and breadth of Africa.

I have to admit that some of the friendliest train journeys I have ever made have been in poor countries where companionship, food and drink are shared with a generosity and courtesy almost unthinkable in the affluent West. Russian trains can be lively parties rolling all through the vodka-fuelled night; it is not only the locomotives that are well oiled. In the open carriages of modern British trains, however, it is easy to fear the worst. "My dear," as the English actor Ernest Thesiger said of his experience as a soldier in the front line during the Battle of the Somme, while trying to get on with the embroidery he had taken with him, "the noise, and the people".

Early railway carriages would have been cramped and noisy; jolting, smelly and spookily dark at night. First Class carriages were basically horse-drawn vehicles mounted on the iron way, and equipped with deep cushions to soften the ride. Second Class passengers would have had a roof over their heads, while the earliest Third Class passengers travelled exposed to the elements.

By the 1870s, US transcontinental trains were comfortable things; George Pullman had made his mark. By the turn of the century, main-line trains in the developed and colonial worlds were often comfortable, too, equipped with corridors, lavatories, hot running water, steam heating and electric light. The dining car was also established by this time, allowing long-distance schedules, free from luncheon stops, to be cut.

Railway carriages were, perhaps, at their finest in the 1930s and 1940s, with trains like the Orient Express, 20th Century Limited and Coronation Scot. I long, though, to have ridden from London to Glasgow over Shap and Beattock, at some time between 1908 and 1914, in the comfort of one of the 12-wheeled, "plum and spilt-milk" liveried composites coaches of the LNWR's 2p.m. express.

Too many train interiors, especially in the age of the DMU and EMU, are dull things, a little too like the Economy Class sections of airliners. Garish fabrics. Harsh lighting. Unmitigated plastic. Claustrophobic lavatories. And windows as sealed as the train that took Lenin from Helsinki to St Petersburg.

↑   How to pour champagne the Pullman car way: a dining car on board the Pacific Railroad, 1870. Just 30 years before this US magazine engraving, passenger trains had been little more than horse carriages and wagons on rails. Very quickly the idea arose that the railway carriage could be a very fine vehicle indeed. What it needed was bogies rather than wheels fixed to rigid chassis, gangway connections from one carriage to another, food and drink. This carriage is designed, very much in the spirit of its times, like a cross between a Victorian drawing room, saloon bar and gentleman's club.

↑   Scene on board an early Pullman car "Holden" running through Illinois in the 1890s. American trains were, initially, way ahead of their European counterparts in terms of ride and comfort. This was most probably because of the vast distances travelled by North American trains, many of them riding through the night, or even over several days and several nights. George Pullman (1831–97) patented his luxurious Pullman Car in 1857. Pullman built a model town for his employees on the edge of Chicago, but died an unpopular man, his grave held down by railway sleepers. These elegant ladies seem content, though.

→   Home from home in the sleeping compartment of an American Pullman, 1905. Just look at those rich timber cabinets, decorative metalwork and heavy cotton sheets and blankets. A mother brushes her daughter's hair before retiring for the night. The sheer degree of comfort and great weight of these carriages encouraged the design of increasingly powerful locomotives. US railroad cars have always been the heaviest in the world, and those classic American-type 4-4-0s would have been quite unable to get trains composed of cars like this on the move, and at any speed. By this time Pullman trains had reached Europe.

↑   Trains were not always as luxurious as Pullmans, even in North America. In the 1890s, a small cluster of bowler-hatted businessman keep a wary eye on the stranger in the soft-hat on board a Canadian Pacific sleeper. Their day seats are made of hard, slatted timber, but no doubt their beds, folded up into the ceiling like the luggage lockers of modern airliners, will be a little more giving. This is clearly a publicity shot from the railroad, but what was it meant to say? Canadian Pacific, the Calvinist road? Say farewell to creature comfort when you step aboard CPRR?

→   Waiter, there's a fly in my soup. Never mind, sir, the spider on the bread roll will get him. A posed scene, from 1905, in the 12-wheeled dining car of a London and North Western express nominally on its way from Euston to Liverpool to catch a ship to America, but probably at rest in the carriage works at Wolverton. Cameras and film were not quick enough to capture live scenes on board such trains. These heavy expresses, powered by small, yet punchy new 4-4-0s, would maintain 55mph schedules while breakfast, lunch, dinner and tea were served in Edwardian quantities.

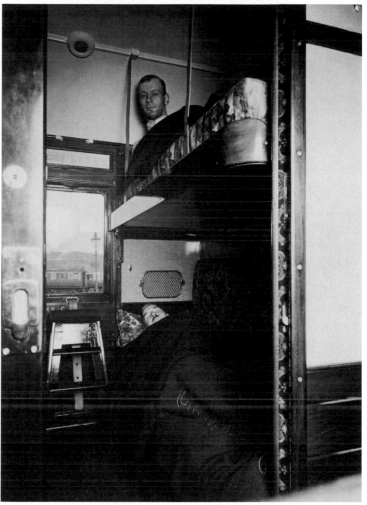

← May I have your bread rolls, too, Maude? This travelling lark has brought on an appetite, I can tell you. Two ample ladies in a sumptuous First Class LNWR diner tuck diligently into an ambitious lunch. The date is 1905, and carriages like these must have been a joy to those who could afford them on the long run up and down to Scotland from Euston. Look at those plush armchairs, cushions stuffed with horsehair, leather armrests and starched white antimacassars. Even then, as their clothing suggests, trains could still be draughty, while cinders might fly in through open windows.

↑ LNWR sleeping car, 1905. These were designed to be like miniature Edwardian hotel bedrooms, and do look snug and inviting with all that chintz and plushness. It reminds me of those lovely lines in "Skimbleshanks, the Railway Cat" from T S Eliot's *Old Possum's Book of Practical Cats*, describing a sleeping compartment on the Anglo-Scottish Night Mail from Euston: "There was every sort of light, you could make it dark or bright/And a button you could turn to make a breeze/And a funny little basin you're supposed to wash your face in/And a crank to shut the window should you sneeze."

↑ Reportage photograph of one man sound asleep, another up top looking mighty suspicious – can't trust these photographer johnnies – on a Great Western sleeping car express, August 1928. These chaps are travelling Third Class, and do not seem too badly off for it. They are probably bound from Paddington to Plymouth, or the other way around, as many servicemen would have been at the time. Their locomotive is likely to be a four-cylinder Star or Castle 4-6-0, both of which will give a smooth ride once they have gathered speed, their crisp exhaust, a railway lullaby, resounding through the night.

← A scene on board a cinema car somewhere in the US. The film is silent, unlike the train, so we're still in the 1920s. The first "talkie" feature was *The Jazz Singer* (Alan Crosland, 1927). Today, on long train journeys, passengers (sorry, "customers") pout and sulk in their own private worlds as they listen to thumpa-whoompa music on personal stereos. Train travel was very different when passengers sat down like this to watch a film together. Did cinema cars survive long enough for these chaps to gawp at The 20th Century Limited disappearing into a tunnel as Hitchcock's stars clinched?

↙↙ Take a memo, Miss Jones. You mean a wax cylinder recording, Sir Ernest? Whatever. Here, in 1934, a British captain of industry works, grappling with a speaking tube, as an LNER express thunders down to King's Cross from Edinburgh and North East England in the charge of a Gresley three-cylinder A1 or A3 Pacific. This mobile office, in days long before the dreaded mobile phone ("I'm on the train"), was a service provided by a number of railways. Urgent messages could be handed to telegraph boys at intermediate stations and relayed by wire to their destination ahead of the fleetest express.

↙ It's the way he tells them. Flappers travelling in a Jersey Central observation car, leaning forward to hang on to every word of a spruce businessman seeing just how wide he can spread his legs to impress the ladies. The date is 1930, just before the revolution in design that led to trains like the Henry Dreyfuss edition of the 20th Century Limited. This car is modelled on a liner, with its cane seats and open-air balcony. It must have been an enjoyable way of travelling. I wonder what a balcony on the back of a Eurostar would be like?

↓ Don't fancy yours much. English businessmen settle down to serious drinking in an experimental "tavern car" introduced on the Southern Region of the newly nationalised British Railways in May 1949. The coach was meant to look like and capture the atmosphere of the archetypal English village pub. Except for the fact that everyone got drunk, it did no such thing. The guard rails at the table edges are a good thing; British trains have long bucked and swayed at speed, and not even these cheery chaps wanted a pint of Bass or a mixed grill spilt down their trouser leg.

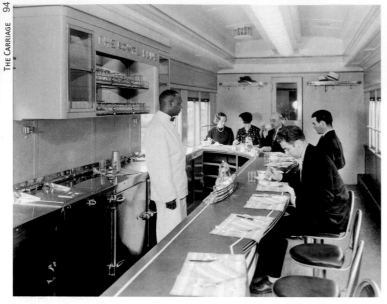

←← Respectful diners at the counter of a brand new Reading streamliner, United States, 1937. This is the moment when industrial designers got to grips with the train, which is why everything – hats, glasses, conversation – is kept neatly in place even as the streamlined Pacific races away up front in dramatic style.

← All these new design trends; where will they all end, I say. Drink your tea and pretend you haven't noticed, dear. A desperately fashionable Art Deco buffet car, designed for otherwise straight-laced Southern Railway EMU services between London Victoria, Bognor Regis, Chichester and Littlehampton, June 1938. It will never catch on.

↙↙ Now, this is more like it. Hard to know how well the mean-faced fellow ogling the would-be Lucille Ball Hollywood starlet across the gangway will do, but at least he and his fellow passengers will dine well. This is an informal diner on board the 1948, diesel-hauled edition of the New York Central's 20th Century Limited, from New York to Chicago, designed by Henry Dreyfuss. Compare this to the SR buffet car above: a case of dry Martini cocktails or hard cheese. Note the use of concealed lighting, comfortable seating, confident, restrained décor, and, although you cannot feel it, effective air conditioning.

↙ You don't say? Is that how many bucks it costs to get them to go away? Passengers on board a US express in January 1938 face up to the horrid truth: this trio is going to bother them just as they were ready to eat. These, though, are not buskers, but musicians contracted by the railroad. Throughout the 1930s, US railroads dreamed up ways of entertaining passengers. This had to be better than listening to some selfish, open-mouthed bore's personal stereo. Everyone wears smart clothes, and indeed most people did, rich or poor, until the triumph of leisurewear 50 years later.

↓ Now, then, go easy, young Miss; that's your third already and we've only got to Slough. Wary steward serves vampish lady in a brand new Great Western buffet car, September 1938. The idea of informal eating and drinking like this was new in Britain, and must have seemed especially so on the trains of a four-square railway like the Great Western. Yet, for all its well-ordered Edwardian looks, the GWR ran some of the fastest and best equipped European main line trains of the 1920s and 1930s. These posing passengers, at Swindon Works, look very much up to the minute.

↖ Gee, mommy, I reckon that man over there has just poisoned his wife. Now, honey, just finish your Butterscotch Sundae, and we'll get some sleep. This is the main dining car of the 1948 20th Century Limited. It is a truly refined design, offering its lucky clients an impressive menu: Bisque of Crab Cardinal, Roast Long Island Duckling with Celery Dressing, Filet of Fresh Gaspe Salmon Saute. This hotel on wheels was inaugurated on September 15, 1948 by General Eisenhower. Eight years later, as US President, he was to sign the Interstate Highway Act that helped destroy these superb trains.

← Don't eat the melon — I just spat in it. Addams family-style daughter catches the eye of a kindred soul in the elevated, tinted-windowed restaurant of this General Motors concept train of 1947. The diesel-hauled, air-conditioned express was off on a tour of principal US cities at a time when the railroads were investing heavily in new design and technology. It was a brave effort. There is no question that this would have been an enjoyable and comfortable way to travel, but the railroads were to lose money on their investment as passenger trains gave way to highways and airliners.

↑ Hey, I know, let's invent the Carry On films. Not now, Sidney — this is 1936, and I want to catch up with the latest *Picture Post*. Holiday makers having a laugh in a Great Western camping coach. This was one way of employing carriages and making them pay, if all else failed: should the car and plane appropriate their business. In fact, these camping coaches — there were some 200 located at 160 destinations in Britain before the Second World War — were seen as a good public relations initiative. These chaps would have surely have gone on holiday by train anyway.

Overleaf left → → Okay, who stole my husband? Publicity shot of the interior of the observation car at the tail end of the 1948 20th Century Limited. This car ran until 1968 when the legendary train finally gave up the ghost. Again, note how people were expected to dress half a century ago.

Overleaf right → → The gamine look is in as this Pennsylvania split-level car takes to the road in the mid-1950s. The chap, three seats down on the right, is more interested in the cute dame than in this new-generation design, but she seems to have eyes for someone out of camera range.

↓ Try my red cabbage pirogi, comrade. You look as if you have been in a Siberian camp for the past Five-Year Plan. I have, comrade; what do you think I'm doing on the Trans-Siberian Express? Joking aside, these Russian expresses offered decent, fresh and filling food along the length of their odyssean journeys. Tea and vodka were readily available, as, remarkably, was subsidised caviar, a real treat. If you travelled Soft Class, living on board the Trans-Siberian could be a lot better than struggling to do so in many Soviet towns when this picture was taken in 1976.

↓↓ It says here it's the 1960s. Classic early 1960s design in the guise of this Canadian National dining car, dating from 1964. Like the Soviet railways, Canadian railways offered long journeys on trains that wound past lakes, rolled along past boundless wheatfields, crossed mountains and coped with bitterly cold winters. They needed to be spacious and comfortable, and they were. This picture captures, in many ways, the dream of post-war long-distance travel: bright, clean, well serviced and secure. Would you really prefer to drive all the way in January from Calgary to Toronto, when you could cross Canada like this?

↘ While some passengers come and go along the route of the Trans-Siberian Express, others dig in and stick out the entire seven nights. This comrade has just finished a bottle of vodka along with a small mountain of snacks. He has plenty of time to sleep it off, especially as the train, rolling across interminable steppes and through immense forests, rolls along at a steady speed and as smoothly as if it was riding not on steel springs, but air. And, in winter, the cars are as warm as blinis. By this time, 1975, the train would have been electric powered throughout.

↓↓ Comrades playing card games in their four-berth carriage on the Trans-Siberian Express, 1966. These trains were a good place to meet Russians and other Soviet people during the Cold War. If you could hold your drink, play chess, cards, read Dostoyevksy and bear to listen to the balalaika, you were made.

→ This is taking the concept of "loss of face" a little too far. But perhaps these solitary businessmen, staring out at the passing Japanese countryside from a Tokyo-to-Kyoto express, are the passengers of the future: self-contained and wishing to avoid eye, and any other, contact with fellow travellers.

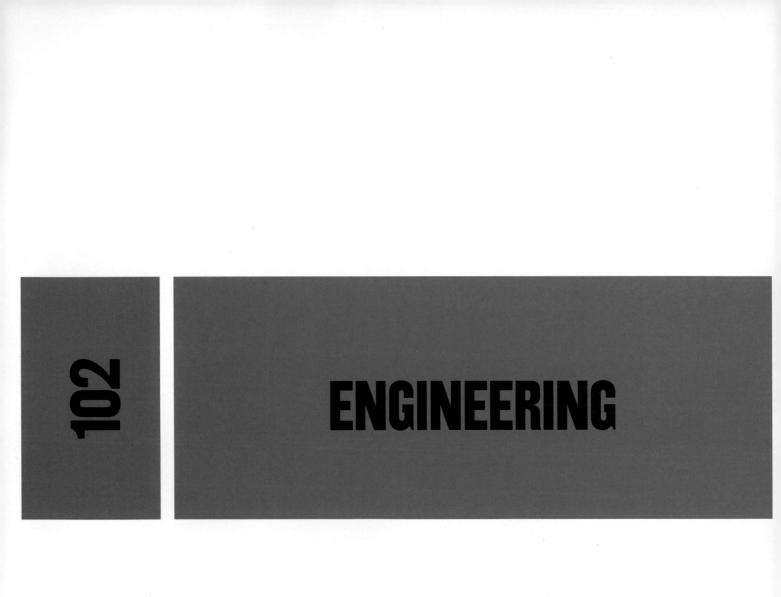

102 ENGINEERING

The speed at which the railway spread was astounding. Victorian railways were like an iron and steel version of today's World Wide Web. By the turn of the 19th century, trains were running across the world, with the fastest capable of 90mph and offering hotel-style accommodation to those who could afford it.

This level of rapidly increasing speed and sophistication was dependent upon robust engineering. To run fast, trains required smooth track, fail-safe signalling and diligent maintenance, as well as locomotives and trains that could roll along efficiently. Because they were such a huge and innovative enterprise, railways employed and trained armies of the best civil and mechanical engineers of their day. Civil engineers surveyed lines, then built and serviced them; mechanical engineers provided the trains themselves.

Whole towns grew up around the greatest railway workshops, such as Swindon and Crewe in England. These became important centres of engineering knowledge and innovation. They were also the training grounds of those who were to become famous in other engineering ventures. W O Bentley, for example, founder and chief designer of the original Bentley Motors (1919–31) and its famous Le-Mans-winning racing cars, had been a premium engineering apprentice at Doncaster with the Great Northern Railway.

Railway engineers designed and built viaducts, bridges, tunnels and cuttings. They built lines across mosses, moors, steppes and deserts. They built other lines across straits, through jungles, up mountains and under the sea. They have given us steam locomotives that have run at 200km/h, and electric trains that can exceed 500km/h. They have developed braking systems that bring the fastest trains safely to a halt in less than a mile. They have made a few mistakes along the way (p110), but on the whole they are unsung heroes of the industrial, and "post-industrial", worlds.

In 2003, BBC TV asked viewers to vote for their all-time favourite Great Briton. Inevitably, perhaps, the winner was Winston Churchill (1874–1965). It was quite remarkable, though, to see Isambard Kingdom Brunel (1806–59), the railway and marine engineer, taking second place. This terrier-like chap, forever fixed in our mind's eye sporting an ambitious cigar and battered stove-pipe hat, dreamed big dreams and built them. He embodied the concept of the fast express train galloping heedlessly and relentlessly across infinite landscapes.

Engineers like Brunel, Eiffel and others have proved that it is possible to build vast engineering projects that enhance, rather than detract from, nature. It is hard for the heart not to be stirred by the Forth Railway Bridge in Scotland (p112), or by the daring railways of Switzerland.

British hearts, sadly, sink when faced by the state of their own degraded main line railways at the outset of the 21st century. Here, decades of railway engineering have been frittered away to satisfy politicians' unhealthy obsession with the dogma of privatization and deregulation at all costs, up to and including the derailment of express trains and the cruel deaths of their passengers. From 1997, the maintenance of tracks, a skill handed down from generation to generation, was fobbed off to firms of contractors for whom railways were just as uninteresting as any other routine maintenance work. As long as the companies could get their corporate noses into the deepening trough of government subsidy, they were happy.

The results of this cynical political stratagem have been pathetic. Railway engineers ought to be able to work, with quiet passion and knowledgeable enthusiasm, to produce the best and safest railways we can afford, as they once did, and still do in many parts of the world, as this chapter shows.

↖↖ Teenage boys disregard *Acheron* as this Gooch Firefly 2-2-2 steams out of a barley-sugar tunnel mouth between Bath and Bristol, 1846. The dog seems indifferent, too. Only the chap in the tall hat appears to be awatre of the railway revolution unfolding before them; he is probably a Church of England vicar. The Great Western main line from London to Bristol (1835–41) was engineered by Isambard Kingdom Brunel (1806–59); the construction of tunnels was the greatest challenge to early railway engineers. It is no wonder they sought to endow their work with architectural grandeur like this. Accurate lithograph by John Cooke Bourne (1814–96).

↖ Infernal scene showing the construction of the two-mile-long Kilsby Tunnel near Rugby on the London and Birmingham Railway, 1837. The work is done by navvies, horses, explosives and Robert Stephenson (1803–59). John Cooke Bourne captured the sublime aspect of this great engineering work. A shaft of sunlight penetrates one of two ventilation shafts opened through the bore of the tunnel. Without these, smoke from locomotives would have generated dangerous gases, while the atmosphere would have been obnoxious to passengers and train crews. The change of air pressure caused by the shafts can be felt inside smokeless electric expresses today.

← Coloured engraving of Edge Hill, Liverpool & Manchester Railway, 1830. The railway was engineered by George Stephenson. It faced two major obstacles. The first was crossing Chat Moss, a bog that threatened to suck *Rocket* and her siblings into the underworld. The second was the entry to Liverpool, cut through a mile or more of the tsame red sandstone used to build Sir Giles Gilbert Scott's Liverpool Cathedral in the 20th century. Early trains were dwarfed by this impressive engineering work, which today's electric trains still pass through on the final leg of their journey from Edge Hill to Liverpool.

↑ None of these fine folk, nor their dogs – much less the seagulls wheeling over fishing smacks, bobbing on the Menai Straits – pay the slightest bit of attention to a small 2-2-2 locomotive as it scurries with a train out of Robert Stephenson's Conway Bridge, linking Anglesey and mainland Wales on the Chester to Holyhead line. The enclosed bridge, formed of two 412ft rectangular iron tubes, ran between mock medieval gateways right in front of historic Conway Castle. The bridge was opened in 1849. The coloured lithograph was made by Newman & Co from a drawing by John Lister Jr.

↑ This is the first train to run on the Circum-Baikal Railway, Siberia, along the great freshwater lake in 1904. This beautiful line runs the 84km from Khultuk to Port Baikal. Originally part of the Trans-Siberian railway, a new line from Irkutsk to Slyndyanka relegated it to a branch line in the 1950s. But as an engineering feat, it is a marvel. Its construction involved 424 major engineering works, including 39 tunnels and 14km of stone supporting walls. Trains run through numerous galleries to guard them from snow and rockfalls. It is a terrific journey, although there are few trains. Life on the railway today is as bucolic as it was for these languid looking state railway workers a century ago.

→ British Columbia joined Canada in 1871 with the promise of a rail link from Vancouver to Calgary, and so east to Toronto, Montreal and Ottowa. It was easier said than done. This is a wild and mountainous landscape, the haunt of grizzly and black bears. The Canadian Pacific's dynamic new general manager, William Cornelius Van Horne, appointed in 1882, was adamant. The following year his "manager of construction", James Ross engineered a spectacular line over the Rogers Pass. This is the breathtaking timber trestle bridge that Ross built over Mountain Creek, 331m long and 50m above the torrent below. It seems to be built of matchsticks; it was strong enough, but has long been replaced.

Overleaf →→ A fine 1859 photograph showing construction of Brunel's Royal Albert Bridge over the Tamar River at Saltash, Cornwall, for the Great Western Railway. The bridge, very much in use today, is approached on steep curves. Its centre is composed of two massive elliptical iron trusses, like great eyes gazing out, with utter confidence, over the river. The portals rightly bear Brunel's imposing name in massive letters. This image reveals the dramatic impact the arrival of the railways had on rural Britain. What did the people living in the handsome houses at the foot of this leviathan make of it? They probably had no say, and would soon get used to Great Western Expresses rumbling over one of Brunel's finest works.

↑ "Beautiful Railway Bridge of the Silv'ry Tay!/Alas! I am very sorry to say/That ninety lives have been taken away/On the last Sabbath day of 1879,/Which will be remember'd for a very long time." William McGonagall's "Tay Bridge Disaster" is one of the great comic verses of Scottish literature. It was not meant to be funny. It just is. The collapse of the Tay Bridge, Dundee, the longest single-span bridge in the world at the time, was not funny either. Engineered by Sir Thomas Bouch for the North British Railway, it opened on May 31, 1878. Describing an elegant arc, as if drawn by a single sweep of a pen, it does look a bit flimsy. But this is hindsight; no one knew at the time.

↗ "When the train left Edinburgh/The passengers' hearts were light and felt no sorrow/But Boreas blew a terrific gale/Which made their hearts for to quail/And many of the passengers with fear did say/I hope God will send us safe across the Tay." He didn't. At 7.15p.m. a six-coach North British Railway Edinburgh-Dundee express crossed the bridge during a Force 10–11 gale, at the same time as Bouch's structure gave way. "As soon as the catastrophe came to be known/The alarm from mouth to mouth was blown/And the cry rang out all o'er the town/Good Heavens! the Tay Bridge is down." In this engraving for the *Illustrated London News* (January 3, 1880), steam launches and a diver's barge search for survivors.

→ A chappie with a bulldog expression poses with the North British locomotive that plunged off the Tay Bridge and into the firth. It is a Wheatley 4-4-0. The locomotive was rescued and put back into service. Crews called her "The Diver". The Tay Bridge disaster remains Britain's most catastrophic civil engineering failure. Bouch had been knighted after the bridge's completion but, after the events of the last Sabbath day of 1879, his reputation collapsed. At the time he was working on designs for the even more ambitious Forth Railway Bridge (p112). The commission was handed over to Benjamin Baker and Sir John Fowler. McGonagall recommended buttresses in future bridge design,

"For the stronger we our houses do build/The less chance we have of being killed."

THE FORTH BRIDGE.

CAGE FOR BUILDING BOTTOM M

MARCH 9. 1887

← Opened in March 1890, the tremendous cantilevered Forth Railway Bridge remains one of the marvels of engineering and railway worlds. Designed by Baker and Fowler, it is 1.5 miles long, contains 54,000 tons of steel, took eight years to construct and was the biggest bridge in the world. It spans the Firth of Forth, connecting Edinburgh to Fife, and created a short-cut route for trains travelling from London and Edinburgh to Aberdeen. In March 1887, workers are seen erecting a steel cage within which the main structural member of one of the bridge's vast trusses is beginning to take shape.

↑ Some while later, and the stupendous structure of the Forth Bridge is all but revealed. It could be seen from central Edinburgh, and when completed, was a joy to travel over. The trains that do so today seem like toys. Famously, gangs are employed throughout the year to paint the bridge from one end to the other, to combat rust. On its centenary, a special train hauled by Gresley A4 Pacific 60009 *Union of South Africa* steamed across Baker and Fowler's tour de force; it has always looked its best with trails of steam wafting through its riveted girders.

↑ A massive, movable timber framework is erected in the mid-1860s to allow these men to construct the daring, single span, iron and glass roof of St Pancras station, London. The biggest of its kind in the world at the time, it measured 100ft high and 240ft wide. The train shed was designed by William Barlow. The iron ribs were made at the Butterley Company, Derbyshire, and transported directly to this construction site by the Midland Railway's new London extension. These ribs rise directly from the platform floor, which ties them down and keeps them stable. Barlow's masterpiece is currently being renovated.

→ Barlow's train shed in all its glory. This busy Edwardian scene shows horse-drawn Hansom cabs as well as early motor taxis lined up to take businessmen from Manchester, Sheffield and the Midlands to meetings and plump luncheons in central London. The Midland Railway trains are dwarfed by this heroic structure. Its roof peaks in an almost Gothic fashion, appropriate given the Gothic Revival hotel that fronts it. Note the function of the high roof: to dissipate steam and smoke. Barlow's design was hugely influential and much visited by rival European engineers who did their best to outdo him.

↑ A switching station, or turntable, on the Canadian National Railways, Montreal, Quebec, 1960. Railways and their locomotives threw up all sorts of challenges for engineers. How best might locomotives be housed, serviced and, in the case of tender engines, turned? This satisfying, star-shaped turntable allows locomotives to move from a shed arranged around the edge of a circle to a wide choice of tracks. The engine can be turned by hand if necessary, and by one man, although by this time heavy-duty turntables like this one were powered by steam from the locomotives themselves. This powerful two-cylinder locomotive is one of a highly successful series of CN U2 Confederation class

4-8-4s – this one is U2-c 6153, built at the Montreal Locomotive Works in 1929.

↗ The Garabit viaduct, poised like a ballerina over the River Truyere in the Massif Central, France, is the finest bridge designed by Gustave Eiffel (1832–1923), best known for the tower that bears his name in Paris. The wrought iron bridge is extremely light but stable, and is painted a striking shade of red. At over 400ft, it was the highest bridge in the world when it opened in 1884. It is 1,853ft long and a worthy successor to the great brick Roman aqueduct at Nimes that had, until then, been the most impressive engineered structure to span the French landscape. Eiffel built bridges for railways from Peru to Vietnam, and designed Budapest's Nyugati station (1879).

→ The Ribbleshead Viaduct at Settle, North Yorkshire, in March 1983 at a time when British Rail wanted to abandon the spectacular Settle and Carlisle line, of which this brick structure is the single most impressive engineering feature, while English Heritage wanted to conserve it. Luckily it has survived; steam specials still cross the Victorian viaduct today on their way over Batty Moss between Leeds and Carlisle. The viaduct, built entirely of brick, was completed over five years, from 1870 to 1875, during which many of the navvies toiling on its construction died. It has 24 arches. It is 440 yards long, 104ft high and deeply impressive. The glum little DMUs that trundle across it daily are no match for its grandeur.

← Nearing completion in the early 1990s, this is the vast Eurotunnel terminal near Folkestone, Kent. Very soon, Eurostar trains will be diving under the 30-mile Channel Tunnel here on their way to Lille, Brussels and Paris. A tunnel linking England and France had been a dream of engineers from the 18th century. The military ambition of Napoleon Bonaparte put paid to the earliest projects. The tunnel was only finally opened in 1994. The infrastructure built around the Eurotunnel services was enormous. Cars, lorries and coaches are ferried on special sealed, locomotive hauled trains and run all day in between the 300km/h passenger services. The tunnel consists of three concrete tubes, two for rail tracks and a third as an emergency escape route and service duct.

↑ Horseshoe Curve is a highly distinctive, and grand, feature along the Pennsylvania Railroad route from New York to Chicago. It skirts the Altoona Reservoir, and is seen here in a spectacular publicity shot from October 21, 1954, the curve's centenary, and, by chance, the 75th anniversary of the incandescent light bulb. A pair of diesel expresses cross paths bathed in a surreal glow, which, according to the Sylvania Electric Products Company, was the equivalent of 15 million 60-watt bulbs. This was the stomping ground of great Pennsy trains like the *Broadway Limited*, which in its 1940s heyday was hauled by the stunning Raymond Loewy-styled, Altoona built, T-1 4-4-4-4s, some of the fastest and most powerful locomotives ever built. Imagine watching one pacing around Horseshoe Curve.

Overleaf →→ I am not sure if you can really see the Great Wall of China from the Moon, but we can be sure that the path of the Trans-Siberian Railway, 5,778 miles from Moscow to Vladivostok, is clearly visible from outer space. This awe-inspiring photograph was taken on April 12, 1994 from the NASA Space Shuttle *Endeavour*. The dark hub near the centre is Omsk. The railway was built over very many years. The section from Lake Baikal to Vladivostok (1908–14) was the most demanding, costing the lives of thousands of exiles and prisoners, navvies and engineers. Today the line is exceptionally busy; it is a major route for container traffic from the Far East to Europe as well as an essential passenger line.

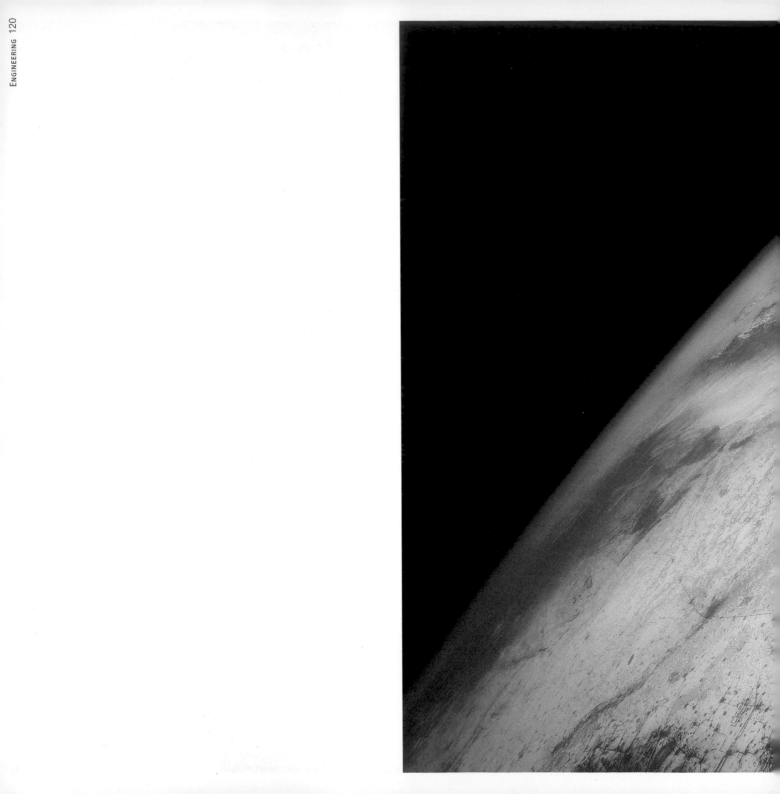

ARCHITECTURE

It was the world's first trunk line from Birmingham Moor Street to London Euston, opened in 1838, that did it – that brought imposing architecture to the railways. These railway pioneers saw themselves as industrial age successors to ancient Greeks and Romans. Where the Greeks enhanced natural landscapes with temples and Romans built arrow-straight roads and aqueducts across the impossible reaches of their empire, so the Victorians built the railways, their viaducts, tunnels and stations.

If they built these in the guise of Greek or Roman public buildings, it was because they wanted them to smack of history, learning and grandeur. The Euston Arch suggested that the railways were far more than a rattly ride from "The Smoke" (London) to the "Workshop of the World" (Birmingham) behind a 10-ton Bury 2-2-0. This classical tradition continued into the 20th century, reaching its zenith, if not the buffer stops, with Penn and Grand Central stations, New York.

Architectural fashions came and went with the speed of express trains between the 1830s and First World War. Railway architecture changed with them. Or at least they did in terms of major buildings. What the railways also helped to invent was a humbler, but ultimately highly influential, form of design, the mass-produced or pre-fabricated building.

This made sense. Along the course of ever lengthening railways, there would be many stations, depots and houses for staff. These needed to be built cheaply and efficiently; it made sense to keep them in one easily recognizable and easily built style.

If you look at photographs of stations that once ran up the old Great Central line from London Marylebone to Nottingham Victoria, you will see how this, the last main line to London, had standardized its architecture to a high degree.

State-owned railways elsewhere in the world did much the same; scores of stations in Russia, Finland and Prussia, for example, are much the same as the next one down the line.

Main line terminuses, however, came to be seen not just as stone and marble advertisements for individual railway companies, but as gateways to the cities they served. They remain so much more special than airports, no matter how impressive the architecture of individual terminals, because they are at the hub of the city centre; sometimes they are the hub.

Much of the best loved railway architecture dates from before the Second World War, although there has been good railway architecture since. Sadly, because many fine stations are in city centres, there has been a tendency to hem them in or smother them in fast-buck office blocks, or "rent slabs". In a deeply insensitive, profiteering development at Charing Cross, London, in the late 1980s, platforms were buried under the bulk of a gimcrack Post-Modern office block. The peevish response of architects and developers to critics was that since the station was served exclusively by electric trains, there was no need for high, glass-roofed train sheds. Why, then, do the latest European stations, served by electric trains, boast high roofs? Because, they make us all walk taller; because they match the lofty nature of the trains they serve; and because we all need to breathe a little in crowded cities.

Railway architecture, which reached its nadir worldwide between 1960 and 1990, is on the rise again. There are fine new stations on the TGV line to Marseilles, an imposing new central station under construction in Berlin, an impressive renovation and extension of St Pancras, London, and a heroic new station in Florence. Theatres of everyday life, railway stations deserve to be lovingly designed whatever their style.

Overleaf ← ←
The building of the Parthenon in
Ancient Greece? No, this is the
Greek-style propylaeum, better
known as the Euston Arch, under
construction in London, 1837.
Queen Victoria is about to ascend
the throne, and the London and
Birmingham Railway, the world's
first long-distance passenger line,
will soon open. The railways saw
themselves as the industrial age
inheritors of ancient Greek and
Roman mantles. They would excel
these lauded cultures in style and
engineering prowess. What better
way to arrive or depart one
of the world's greatest cities than
through such heroic portals?
Contemporary watercolour by
John Cooke Bourne.

← The Euston Arch, completed
at a cost of £35,000 in 1838, before
the First World War. Standing 72ft
tall, this immense Doric gateway
was designed by Philip Hardwick
(1792–1870), architect of
Birmingham Cathedral, a man
who understood the cultural as
well as the economic importance
of the new railways. Tragically, the
arch was demolished, despite
much protest, between November
1961 and February 1962 to make
way for the grim and undignified
station that serves passengers
from Euston today. As with the
demolition of Penn Station, New
York, this act of puerile
philistinism fuelled an emerging
conservation lobby.

↑ An official LMS photograph
from the mid-1920s showing Sir
George Gilbert Scott's Midland
Grand Hotel, fronting St Pancras
station, London, in all its
Gormenghast-like Gothic glory. A
magnificent addition to the
London skyline, Scott's hotel was
all but out of date even as it
opened in 1874. With coal fires in
every room, and an army of
scuttling servants, it was
uneconomical and considered
old-fashioned. Closed in 1935, it
became railway offices.
Threatened several times with
demolition, it is now being
renovated as a hotel and flats as
part of the new Eurostar terminal.

← The imperious Roman-style concourse of Pennsylvania station, New York, when brand new in 1910. Based partly on the Baths of Caracalla, this was one of the most imposing and ambitious railway stations ever built. "Was", sadly, is the key word. In an act of childish petulance, the station was demolished in 1963 to make way for a shabby new office development built over a new station that had no style whatsoever. A cathedral of the railway age had become a public toilet for the era of the automobile. As with the demolition of the Euston Arch, London, this callous act gave new importance to the conservation lobby in the US, and, from then on, historic city buildings of this importance and quality were listed and all but safe from demolition. Penn station was a true masterpiece, designed by McKim Meade and White. This sensational concourse stood behind a long, colonnaded street façade, and led across and down to two tiers of platforms. This is where great trains like the *Broadway Limited* departed on their dramatic runs across the Alleghenies to Chicago and the Mid-West. The 1960s station is now being replaced by a far more appropriate design by SOM architects.

↑ Sealed off in 1981, the abandoned Union Station, Washington DC, was in a very sorry state before Congress voted to renovate this imposing Beaux-Arts design by Daniel Burnham. "Make no small plans" was this big-spirited Chicagoan architect's maxim: when it opened in 1907, Union Station was, inevitably, the world's biggest. This is the great concourse photographed in 1995, seven years after the completion of the new works under the architectural direction of Benjamin Thompson Associates. The station — which once boasted a Turkish bath, bowling alley and mortuary — now features a nine-screen cinema, 120 shops, cafés, bars, restaurants, parking for 1,500 cars and the headquarters of Amtrak. And trains, too. A huge success, it is difficult to think of quite how it was considered fit for demolition 25 years ago. The problem, as for most US railroad buildings realised on this considerable scale, was that of the dramatic decline in long-distance passenger traffic from the late 1950s, with the debut of jet airliners. The scale of Union Station is hard to grasp until you learn the fact that, if it was laid on its side, the Washington Monument would fit quite happily under the coffered vaults of its great concourse.

↓ My father was born in Lahore. My grandfather was an Indian Army officer and, for the British, Lahore was a garrison town guarding the approaches to the Khyber Pass and North West Frontier. Built soon after the Indian Mutiny of 1857, the station was designed, by William Brunton, to be a fortress in time of trouble. Steel doors could seal the interior of this fairy tale building. Maxim guns would fire through slits in its walls. The station was, tragically, the scene of dreadful slaughter at the time of partition in 1947 when Muslims, Hindus and Sikhs massacred one another.

↘ Designed in yellow sandstone, granite and blue-grey basalt as a distant echo of Gilbert Scott's Gothic hotel frontage at St Pancras in London, Victoria station, Bombay (officially, Mumbai today) was the work of Frederick William Stevens. It was built between 1878 and 1888, Queen Victoria's Golden Jubilee. Here it is in the 1980s fronted by red double-deck buses and stately Hindustan Ambassador taxis, based on the 1954 Morris Oxford. These still make this gloriously exaggerated building seem like some 19th-century diplomat from London, but with a dome, based on Tom Tower, Christ Church, Oxford, in place of a sola topi.

Overleaf left →→ *Voici la locomotive. Elle est dans la place.* Accident at Montparnasse station, Paris, October 22, 1895: the Granville-Paris express in charge of 2-4-0 721 forgets to brake. Ploughing through the buffer stops, and across the station's 30-metre concourse, it shoots through this wall and lands on its nose in the Place de Rennes. This is the second Gare Montparnasse, built, 1848–52, in a chaste Roman style. Rebuilt after the Second World War, it was replaced completely, with a 200-metre office tower on top, between 1969 and 1972. The Germans surrendered Paris to General Leclerc here in August 1944.

Overleaf right →→ Le Train Bleu is a Belle Epoque restaurant at Gare de Lyon, Paris. Here it is in 2002, unchanged from the day it opened in 1901. This gorgeous interior was the work of the station's architect, Marius Toudoire, in association with 30 artists commissioned to paint scenes of towns served by the PLM (Paris-Lyon-Marseilles Railway). The station is a riot of sculpture. Only in fin-de-siècle Paris could statues of naked nymphettes be said to symbolize the virtues of technology. Today, the station is served by TGVs that can get to Lyon during the course of a meal at Le Train Bleu.

↑   Of all the sights in Florence, Santa Maria Novella station, designed by Giovanni Michelucci (1891–1991) is among the finest. Opened in 1936, it was heralded as a great Fascist achievement, the sort of station where Mussolini's trains would arrive on time. Yet it is as timeless as modern architecture gets, a rational updating of a Roman basilica stripped of ornament. The play of horizontals, wide stairs and long canopies, however, infuse it with a railway age dynamism. Today, the British architects Foster and Partners are adding a huge new underground concourse alongside Michelucci's masterpiece for a new generation of high-speed trains.

→   Thank you, waiter; I'll have blinis to start, followed by stuffed cabbage, and the ceiling for pudding. This is the sublime restaurant in the gloriously over-the-top Kazansky station, Moscow (1912–26), seen here, in former times, when the Soviet Union still had another 13 years to run its course, and food in Moscow, when you could find it, was cheap and filling. This is the biggest station in Moscow; its architecture, designed by Alexei Shchusev, is a medley of the historic buildings of Kazan. After a vodka, or three, take the train from here to the Volga region, Middle Asia or Kazakhstan.

↖ Union Station, Los Angeles, photographed in 1990. This beautiful Spanish Colonial Art Deco terminus is one of the most relaxed and elegant in any major US city. Its design and landscaping exude quality. It is effortlessly luxurious and a great place to await a train. It seems a shame, however, that so few long-distance trains arrive and depart from its sun-kissed platforms; local services serve Disneyland. This was once the hub of the great trains of the Southern Pacific, Union Pacific and Santa Fe railroads. The building was designed by John Parkinson and Donald B Parkinson and completed in 1939.

← Built from 1857 during the time of the Russian Grand Duchy, Finnish railways were pretty much state-owned from their inception. Stations were standardised. Much later, when the National Romantic movement, characterised by the music of Jean Sibelius, caught on, and with independence in the air, Finnish architects let rip. Helsinki station – with its magnificent concrete vaults, its lantern-bearing giants and its idiosyncratic decoration – is a masterpiece by Eliel Saarinen (1873–1950), who later emigrated to the US. Completed in 1914, the station is kept in spotless condition; a joy to use. The food here is good, while trains run punctiliously.

↑ This is Waterloo station, London, 1994. The serpentine blue and grey structure is the International Terminal opened that year for Eurostar services to Paris and Brussels via the Channel Tunnel. Designed by Nicholas Grimshaw and Partners, it won instant popularity. After a long break during which new main line stations had aped airport terminals, here was a high, glass-roofed structure recapturing the romance of rail travel. From a technical point of view, high roofs had only been necessary to allow steam locomotives to let off steam and to dissipate smoke; but they were generous and looked good, as did Waterloo International.

Overleaf left →→ In the 1990s, railway architects began to reassess their art. Here, in the design of Lyon-Satolas station for TGVs serving Lyon airport, the Spanish architect-engineer Santiago Calatrava (born 1951) looked to create a balance between the aesthetic virtues of railway stations and air terminals. This long and striking vista evokes a great sense of speed and modernity while remaining an essentially calm space. And, just as the iron and glass train sheds of grand Victorian stations have something of a skeletal air about them – skeletons of newly discovered dinosaurs – so Calatrava has created a concrete rib cage; it feels terrific.

Overleaf right →→ The concrete bridge spanning Lyon-Satolas station, and giving access to the platforms below. In the structure of the columns that support bridge and roof, Calatrava conjures barely constrained forces at work through the building, and in the hugely powerful trains that snake in and out of it below. Calatrava is famous for his bridges, such as the Almillo over the Guadalquivir, Seville (1992), or the Lusitania, spanning the Guadiana, Merida (1991); these, too, like this one here at Lyon, share an anthropomorphic power, as do the SNCF trains themselves; TGVs really do resemble pikes or eels.

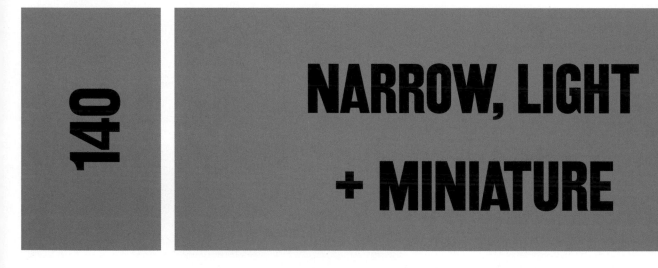

140

NARROW, LIGHT + MINIATURE

A pair of books I treasure tells the story of the Irish narrow-gauge. I missed these railways by a generation. They belonged to a romantic, or poor, Ireland, dead and gone. This was swallowed by a new-found addiction to lorries and cars long before the Celtic Tiger, all fur and no romance, bared its teeth.

How I long to have ridden these often deeply eccentric lines across remote countryside to even remoter ports and market towns. My favourites are the Londonderry & Lough Swilly, the County Donegal (p143), the Listowel & Ballybunion (p144), the Schull & Skibereen (p145) and the Tralee & Dingle. And it would be wrong to forget the impressive NCC (Northern Counties Committee) narrow-gauge corridor boat trains that once ran from Larne to Belfast. Their locomotives were the most handsome express 2-4-4 tanks you will ever have seen; they were also the only express 2-4-4 tank locomotives you could ever have seen.

The names of these railways enjoy a lilting charm that draws you to them like a well-lit, peat-fired, music-haunted Irish pub. What seems so very sad is that if they had survived one more generation, they would be running today, much like the narrow-gauge railways of north Wales; not as essential services, but as popular tourist attractions.

I am, though, kidding myself, because for all the charms of preserved railways, they are something else altogether from the Irish narrow-gauge. Day-trippers reach them by car. They sport baseball caps and trainers, photograph everything in sight with digital cameras, eat as if there were no next meal, and squabble with fractious children.

The Irish narrow-gauge I miss is a world of cattle trains ambling alongside the road to Dingle on market days. Of trains of men in thorn-proof tweeds, keen-eyed sheepdogs beside their boots. A world where shopping malls, call centres, theme parks, leisure centres and tourism would only ever exist in some parallel, future and unthinkable universe.

Luckily, there are railways, a little like the Irish gauge, alive and, if not always steaming, then burbling along 45 years after the closure of the Co Donegal Railways. There are the Cuban sugar plantations and mills with their veteran US steam locomotives, the workaday steam lines serving Baltic coast resorts in the former East Germany.

At Bad Doberan, you can still ride a narrow-gauge steam train through the narrow high street. There are the serpentine railways of Sardinia, and the quixotic trains that skirt the Basque, Asturian and Galician coasts on their six-and-three-quarter-hour crawl from Irun through Bilbao and Santander to Gijon.

There are, too, entire national networks like the South African Railways that run on narrow-gauge track. And then there are miniature railways. To enthusiasts, these are like toy breeds to dog owners. There are curiosities designed as playthings for wealthy enthusiasts, such as the 15-inch Romney Hythe and Dymchurch Railway (p153), Kent, a one-third scale representation of the LNER's east coast main line from London to Edinburgh as it was in the 1920s. There are, too, grand model railways like the 7 1/2-inch gauge Great Cockcrow Railway, chaired by the railway publisher Ian Allan (born 1921), near Chertsey, Surrey. Here men and women, with dogs in tow, spend weekends pottering happily with exact miniatures of some of the finest British steam locomotives.

I might have included model railways, but these, although delightful, are a bit of a cheat. Steam locomotives powered by electricity? Actually there was a small number of steam-electric hybrid shunting locomotives in Switzerland, but theirs is another story. Model railways are also too small to ride, although leprechauns might disagree.

↓ "Rough sea over electric railway, Kemptown, Brighton" reads the caption of this splendid photograph taken soon after the opening of the Volk's Electric Railway at Brighton, the fashionable south coast resort. It seems remarkable that the frail-looking train could brave such elements, but here it is, as it has been, more or less, since it first opened on August 3, 1883 taking daytrippers on a one-mile joy ride along Brighton's imposing Regency promenade. The importance of the Volk's Electric Railway is that it was very probably the first of its kind. It was not a tramway, but a proper railway, albeit a miniature one, up and running within four years of Siemens & Halske's

demonstration of the world's first practical electric train, able to draw current from a third rail, obviating the need for batteries. Magnus Volk was the son of a German clockmaker. A gifted electrical engineer, he came to local prominence when he lit Brighton Pavilion. He rebuilt his railway just a year after it opened, widening its gauge and introducing a much-improved train. He died, aged 86, in 1937. His endearing railway still runs every summer, when the weather can be a little less wild than this.

→ The County Donegal was an extensive narrow-gauge railway that fanned out from Londonderry across remote bogs, glens, mountains and coastlines. Its lines were riddled with steep curves and frequent gradients of one in 60 to one in 40. It served poor, isolated, rural communities, and in its own way it was a success. The fact that it endured to the end of 1959, given competition from lorries and cars, was due to the forward thinking of its best known general manager, Henry Forbes. Forbes bought and commissioned petrol railcars for the lightest traffic; they were much cheaper to run than the CDR's steam locomotives. Here is Number 1, a 10-seater built by Allday and Onions in 1906, at the

CDR's centre of activities at Stranorlar. Her power was uprated from 10hp to 36hp over the years, so she could pull a coach. Today she is preserved at the Ulster Folk and Transport Museum, Cultra, Co Down. But, although well known for its many railcars, the very last County Donegal train arrived in Stranorlar at 8.21p.m. on December 31, 1959 behind a steam locomotive, No 5, a 2-6-4 tank built by Nasmyth Wilson & Co, a year after the No 1 railcar.

ROUGH SEA OVER ELECTRIC RAILWAY, KEMPTOWN, BRIGHTON

↑ In Algeria, the French engineer Charles Lartique observed how well camels carried panniers slung on either side of their humps. This was the inspiration for the Lartique-system monorail. It was first applied in Kerry on the west coast of Ireland. The nine-mile Listowel and Ballybunion Railway was the world's first commercial monorail. Opened in 1888, it lasted 36 years. The monorails rusted in soft Irish rain, traffic was thin and the line was sabotaged during the Civil War (1921–23). How these twin-boilered locomotives crossed the points is anyone's guess. A section of line has been recreated; it opened in 2003.

↗ A lovely scene on the narrow-gauge Ffestiniog Railway, Tan-y-Bwlch station, north Wales, 1933. This is 0-4-0 tank plus tender *Prince* built by George England, London, in 1863. She is still running today. Built to carry slate from mountain quarries to the coast, at Portmadog, the FR opened in 1836 and was originally horse-drawn. With steam, it was the first narrow-gauge railway to carry passengers. After closure in 1946, it was rescued by enthusiasts and, re-opened in 1954, operates a hugely popular tourist service today. Its locomotives include the wonderful push-me, pull-you double-bogie Fairlies. It is the world's oldest independent railway.

→ A horse and cart photographed by the railway historian H C Casserley overtakes a cow-catching Schull & Skibbereen train, headed by a handsome 4-4-0 tank, at Hollyhill in July 1938. Perhaps the train was a little faster, yet this charming narrow-gauge railway in the south-east of Ireland is best remembered for its farcical opening in 1884. Its first locomotives, tiny 16-ton 0-4-0 tanks from Dick, Kerr, proved virtually unable to move themselves, let alone work a train. The visiting railway inspector was not impressed. The 15-mile line finally closed in 1947 as road competition got the better of it.

Narrow, Light + Miniature 145

In 1852 the wealthy Chicago meat-packer Sylvester Marsh got lost climbing the 6,288ft peak of Mount Washington, New Hampshire. This is the highest peak in the White Mountains. It offered a challenge to Marsh. Could he build a railroad to the top? Local politicians laughed and suggested he might as well build a railroad to the Moon. But Marsh was a doer, and he had the last laugh. With the aid of local father and son inventors Herrick and Walter Aiken, Marsh built the world's first cog railway to the top of Mt Washington. The first train was nosed up by *Old Peppersass*, a vertical-boilered engine, now preserved at the railway, on July 3, 1869. The railway has run ever

since. It offers a spectacular journey, by steam, especially up and across Jacob's Ladder, said to be the world's highest and windiest trestle bridge. The gradient here is steeper than one in three; passengers at the front end of the single carriage trains sit 14ft above those at the back. Here is No 2 *Ammonoosuc*, built by Manchester Locomotive Works, New Hampshire in 1875, at work in August 1962. No Washington Cog Railway locomotive is less than 95 years old.

The Siliguri-Darjeeling Railway was declared a Unesco World Heritage Site in 1999. This was wonderful news for the many fans of this narrow-gauge railway. Shortly before this, the Indian Railways had seriously tried to dieselize this famous winding, gyring line, which climbs from a junction with the main line to Calcutta at Silguri, West Bengal, to a summit of 7,500ft at Ghoom, before descending gently into the hill town of Darjeeling. Luckily, the diesels fell off the track on steep curves and were judged a failure. The 2ft gauge railway, with its promise of views of Mt Everest, was built to bring tea down from Darjeeling, and holidaymakers up from the

blazing summer plains below. The journey took three days by packhorse. In its 1930s heyday — seen here — the line was operated by up to 50 locomotives and the journey, with its loops, switch backs, 132 unmanned crossings and gradients of up to one in 23, took just six hours for the 55-mile climb. Today, it is more like 10. Each of these 0-4-0 tanks, built by Sharp Stewart of Glasgow, demands a crew of four: driver, fireman and two sandmen up front helping the engines to keep their grip.

↓   US sanctions against Fidel Castro's Cuba have made life unnecessarily hard in this nominally Communist island. Yet hardship has also encouraged Cubans to improvise, particularly when new technologies are too expensive or where there is neither the fuel nor spare parts to make its use feasible. This is one reason why the island's vital sugar harvest is still collected by large numbers of lovingly kept narrow-gauge US steam locomotives, many of them Baldwin's, like this veteran 2-8-0 hard at work on the 2ft 6in gauge Rafael Freyre Mill in 1996. Another is that engines like this can burn sugar cane.

↘   A Rio Turbio Railway 2-10-2 hard at work in deepest Patagonia with a 60-car freight train in the mid-1990s. This was one of 20 locomotives built by Mitsubishi, Japan, in 1957 to haul coal trains for the most part of the 258km railway between Rio Gallegos and Rio Turbio. Rio Turbio had been founded in 1943 as a coal town. The railway, opened in 1951, was steam operated until 1997. The 750mm-gauge 2-10-2s were modified by the visionary Argentine steam engineer Livio Dante Porta (1922–2003), increasing their power output considerably. They were among the most efficient steam locomotives.

↘↘   A coal-fired steam locomotive working at a paper mill might sound a daft proposition, but it was magical to see this three-mile, 2ft 6in gauge Edwardian railway in action. It was built in 1909 to connect Bowater's Sittingbourne and Kelmsley mills to Ridham Dock on the mournful marshes of the Thames estuary. Its sturdy, apple-green Bagnall and Kerr-Stuart tank locomotives, many equipped, like this one, with a spark arrestor on top of its chimney, worked hard until the line was closed in 1969. A section was re-opened for enthusiasts using seven of the original locomotives. The mills are now Finnish-owned.

→   Italian-built Mallet compound locomotives of the narrow-gauge Eritrean Railway at Asmara. This remarkable 118km railway, built by the Italians during their short-lived African empire, has re-opened after many years of closure. It runs from the Red Sea port, Massawa, across a desert plain before climbing through 30 tunnels and across 60 bridges to reach Asmara, a greater climb than that of Siliguri to Darjeeling in India. The Italian "*serpente d'acciaio*" (steel snake) was taken over by the British in 1942. Largely destroyed during Eritrea's 30-year war with Ethiopia, it has been President Issaias Afewerki's personal ambition to see it re-opened.

← A Garratt locomotive re-imported from South Africa pounds through Snowdonia on the Welsh Highland Railway. The original line, closed to passengers in 1936, had run from Caernarfon to Portmadog, where it met the Ffestiniog Railway. It was part of an ambitious Victorian scheme to create 60 miles of narrow gauge through north Wales. Its story is complex; in short, it failed. Since 1961, enthusiasts have been rebuilding this near mythical railway. With help from the Millennium Commission, it first re-opened in 1997, was extended in 2000, and again in 2003, and is now heading back to the coast at Portmadog.

↙ One of new breed of highly efficient rack railway steam locomotives built for the Brienz Rothornbahn, Zermatt, Switzerland. Designed by Roger Waller, of the AG DLM, formerly a subsidiary of the Sulzer locomotive works, Winterhur, this modern 0-4-2 tank weighs 26 per cent less than its 1930s predecessors, produces 36 per cent more power, is 56 per cent faster while using 41 per cent less fuel. It needs only a driver and its boiler is so well insulated that, left in steam without a fire overnight, it can be up to full working press in 10 to 15 minutes.

↓ The Old Patagonian Express arrives at Esquel, Chubut province, Argentina, 1997. This long, rambling 750cm gauge railway, connecting small towns and barely existent villages in Patagonia, is one of the great survivors. In recent years, it almost ground to a halt. In 2003, however, the Argentine government, 1,000 miles away in Buenos Aires, declared the railway a national monument and provided funding for steam operation throughout its 251-mile length from Esquel to Ingenerio Jacobacci, Rio Negro Province. The twenty-two 2-8-2 locomotives were built equally by Baldwin (USA) and Henschel (Germany). The average speed of this epic journey is 45km/h.

← Well, here's another fine mess; how do you expect me to fit into this cab? Well, I didn't know... Oliver Hardy and Stan Laurel re-open the Romney Hythe and Dymchurch Railway in 1947 after its closure during the Second World War. The comedians were in London when the railway gave them a call. They enjoyed themselves, performing a number of old gags for local people who, while used to the oddity of a miniature main line running past their seaside shacks, would never have expected to see Stan and Ollie in this remote corner of Kent.

↓ The RHDR opened in 1926 to great acclaim. Nigel Gresley, renowned chief mechanical engineer of the LNER, came to the opening to see Henry Greenly's one-third scale replicas of his famous London to Edinburgh A1 Pacifics. These were designed to run at 25mph – a scale 75mph – yet in practice were much faster than this, which would have pleased Captain Howey, the railway's creator, a well-known racing driver. The line, equipped with a fleet of 4-6-2s and 4-8-2s, runs 13.5 miles from Hythe to Dungeness along the Kent coast. More than a tourist attraction, it takes local children to school.

↓ The Wuppertal Schwebebahn, or overhead railway, is one of the most curious forms of city transport in Europe; it is well worth coming this way for the ride. Futuristic in a Jules Verne way, it was championed by a Cologne sugar factory owner, Eugen Langen, and opened in 1901. Its overhead monorail follows the course of the River Wupper, but it also makes forays across the city centre. Here it is in 1951, restored after extensive war damage, thrumming above a horse and cart and Mercedes-Benz truck. The train is formed of stock that has long gone out of service.

↘ The majority of the Class 25s were equipped with condensing tenders that allowed them to run further without water stops. The 25NCs (non-condensing) were a smaller batch; this is 3406, again in June 1978, at Ionia with the 0920 Bethlehem to Bloemfontein. The 25s remained in front-line service until the mid-1980s. One 25NC 3450 was rebuilt by the British engineer David Wardale as the Class 26 *Red Devil*. This was a formidable and highly efficient machine, generating 4,700ihp while using 38 per cent less coal than a standard 25. Management had no interest; it wanted diesels and line closures.

→ Among the fastest and most powerful of all narrow-gauge locomotives were these deep-chested 3,000ihp Class 25 4-8-4s built by Henschel and the North British Locomotive Company, Glasgow for the extensive 3ft 6in gauge South African Railways between 1953 and 1955. Their speed was limited by track engineers, but to see them at 110km/h was a great thrill as they would normally be hauling vast long-distance passenger and freight trains. These were big, free steaming machines well suited to the veldt. This is 25NC 3414, in June 1978, with the daily Bloemfontein to Bethlehem passenger train between Fouriesberg and Sheridan.

CONCEPT TRAINS

August, 1945. Adolf Hitler is dead, the Third Reich destroyed, and Germany occupied by Allied troops. Top Nazi scientists like Werner von Braun and fighter aces who had flown the Me262 jet in combat, such as Major Gunther Rall (275 kills), were packed off to the US for employment or questioning. As far as I am aware, no senior German locomotive engineer was sent with them, but an experimental Deutsche Reichsbahn locomotive was.

This was not some radical turbine-powered locomotive, but DR 19 001, a steam 2-8-2, built in 1935. What on earth would the 757th US Army Railway Shop Battalion want with a pre-war 2-8-2, and why bother to ship it to Fort Monroe, Texas, for examination? Because 19 001 was the world's only V8 steam locomotive, and the V8 engine, a mechanical demi-god, was worshipped in the United States.

Each of the industrial nations developed its own particular design concepts for its railways. The French adored sophisticated compounds. The British did their best to make locomotives that, wheels aside, appeared to have no moving parts. The Americans loved to be shocked and awed by brute power or streamlining.

So while US railroads had developed the steam locomotive to its logical end, in their terms, with highly efficient yet ultimately conventional machines, like the 6,000hp, 110mph Norfolk & Western J class passenger 4-8-4s or the Union Pacific's 6,500hp, 80mph Big Boy freight 4-8-8-4s (p48), the Deutsche Reichsbahn enjoyed experimentation, as did the Luftwaffe.

Conceived by DR's Frederick Witte, with detailed design by Richard Roosen of Henschel, 19 001 was delivered in July 1941. Instead of the conventional arrangement of horizontally mounted cylinders turning the driving wheels through pistons and connecting rods, 19 001 employed eight cylinders arranged in four pairs mounted at 90-degree angles. She ran smoothly and quietly, and,

shrouded in streamlining casing, could outrun most contemporary US V8 sports cars, reaching 117mph. Heavily damaged in a bombing raid on Hamburg in October 1944, and appropriated by US army engineers, she was dispatched to Texas in October 1945. Sadly, 19 001, which served no purpose on US railroads that were rapidly embracing diesel, was scrapped in 1952. The V8 was a tin god but, in the New World, it belonged under the hood of Thunderbirds and Corvettes, not under the running boards of a steam locomotive.

The steam railway locomotive itself had been a concept at the end of the 18th century. This was an era of revolution (France, USA) and technological innovation. Once Richard Trevithick had put James Watt's steam engine on rails and got it to pull wagons with goods and people on board, there was no holding back the tide of railway invention.

Until the diesel lobby got its global grip on the railways, locomotives and trains evolved in an abundance of varieties. In Darwinian fashion, weak designs went to the wall, while the strong survived. Significantly, most of the large-batch production steam locomotives of recent years, notably the Chinese QJ class 2-10-2s (p55), are almost as simple in their construction and mechanical engineering as Stephenson's *Rocket* (p29).

While it would have been fascinating to see Oliver Bulleid's Leader class locomotives (p165) at work in the 1970s, painted in British Rail blue perhaps, what would have been the point in trying to overcome their inherently problematic engineering when a tried and trusted two-cylinder 4-6-0 could do the same work effortlessly and for a fraction of the capital outlay?

This chapter, though, celebrates the wonderful variety of experimental, would-be, and will-be, locomotives and trains, each an attempt to get beyond the basic concepts of Trevithick and Stephenson.

↑ The Philadelphia and Reading's Camelback 4-2-2 378, built by Baldwin in 1896, at Reading station, 1897. The driver's cab is on top of the boiler while the fireman is exposed to the elements behind, shovelling slow-burning waste anthracite into that vast firebox. Camelbacks were devised by John E Wootten (1822–98), a locomotive engineer who became general manager of the Reading system. Anthracite waste was cheap and burned with little or no smoke, but the bulk of the firebox left no room for a conventional cab; hence its odd position. Camelbacks, built from 1877 until 1927, were fast, thrifty machines, and unloved by firemen.

↗ This is Southern Pacific MC-2 class 2-8-8-2 4004 of 1910, the first of many cab-forward Mallet locomotives built for the Southern Pacific. The idea was simple. Pounding through steeply graded tunnels and snow shelters on sharp curves at the head of heavy freight trains on the Sierra Nevada line, long boilers and dense smoke hampered drivers' vision, while threatening crews with asphyxiation. By building the locomotives back to front, the driver had as good a view as he would get from GM and Alco diesel-electrics. Cab forwards became a trademark of the Southern Pacific; they were an all-round success.

→ Less than a year old, the LNER *Hush Hush* locomotive, 10000, departs King's Cross with the non-stop *Flying Scotsman* for Edinburgh, July 31, 1930. This engine was so called because it was designed in great secrecy under the direction of Nigel Gresley. It featured a high-pressure (450psi) marine water-tube boiler, and was a considered a success given its experimental nature. It looked a bit like a whale, and was certainly much bigger than conventional LNER passenger locomotives. It proved expensive to run and was eventually converted into a streamlined A4 Pacific lookalike. Withdrawn in 1959, it was Britain's only 4-6-4.

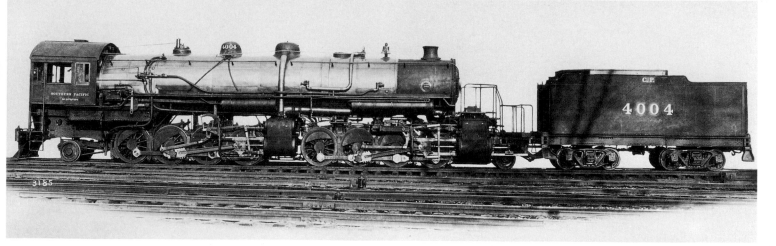

↓ You'll believe a train can fly: here's the Railplane, designed by Scottish engineer George Bennie (1892–1957), ready for take-off at the quarter-mile test track built for it in 1930 at Milngavie, near Glasgow. The white, cigar-shaped Railplane featured nine-foot diameter airscrews fore and aft, and was held in check by an overhead monorail and a guide rail below. It boasted a plush interior, and was much liked by the press, who imagined it running all the way from Scotland to London, silently and without the need for tunnels, at 120mph. Sadly, despite much favourable publicity, Bennie went bankrupt in 1937; the elevated track was dismantled in 1941, and the abandoned Railplane sold for scrap in the 1960s. A 30-minute, two-reeler film dating from 1930 survives in the Scottish Film Archives, serving to remind us of Bennie's brave, blue-sky thinking.

→ You'll believe a Zeppelin can ride the rails: as a change from bombing enemy cities, here is the Zeppelin concept put into high-speed railway service. Invented by Paul Kruckenburg, the starkly appointed, lightweight Rail Zeppelin, or "Schienenzeppelin", was powered by a 600hp BMW aero engine. Along a dead-straight 20km length of track between Hamburg and Berlin, this dramatic machine maintained a maximum speed of 230km/h (142.9mph) on June 21, 1931, a world record on the railways that stood for 20 years. The track had to be straight, because Kruckenburg's flyer would have flown off on bends. It never went into regular service. Its failure has been attributed to the danger of whirling an open propeller about in crowded stations, and to the Deutsche Reichsbahn's own attempt to build a "Fliegende Zeuge", which resulted in the highly successful, air-tunnel tested, two-car, 160km/h (100mph) diesel-electric *Flying Hamburger*, in 1933. Trains *could* fly after all, but along rails, and without the need for propellers.

↓ Well before high-speed tilting trains, engineers were trying to predict the future of trains within the limits of earlier technologies. This is Dr Ing Joseph Hinksen's prototype 200mph monorail train on test at Fuhlingen, Cologne, October 8, 1952. The train was designed to run alongside autobahns, tilting at up to 45 degrees. Fine so long as you weren't going to plump for the pea soup. This 15-metre model represented a full-scale 300-seat passenger train. The idea was never taken up, but it does look convincing, and the idea of trains following motorways might well be worth looking at again.

↓ General Motor's "Train of Tomorrow" toured US cities in the autumn of 1947. This car is divided into family compartments below and an observation gallery above for passengers wanting to watch the world go by. It was no real advance on what had gone before but it looked sleekly sci-fi. It was really a mobile advertisement for GM diesels, which were shortly to push America's steam locomotive manufacturers out of business. Having said this, it would have been great to have been able to sit up on top of this corrugated stainless steel car behind a mighty Hudson or 4-8-4.

→ The three-car Burlington Zephyr was the first streamlined diesel unit in the US. Here the press inspect it on April 17, 1934, the day before it is officially named. Before the Zephyr went into daily service between Lincoln, Omaha and Kansas City, it appeared at the Century of Progress Exposition, Chicago, and toured 222 US cities, where it was seen by two million people while clocking up 30,437 miles. It made a famous publicity dash over the 1,000 miles from Denver to Chicago in 13 hours, at an average speed of 77.6mph, during which it attained a top speed of 112.5mph. The Zephyr is preserved.

↖ This 2,500hp AIA-AIA Brown-Boveri gas-turbine locomotive had a lot to live up to when, as one of two prototypes from Switzerland and England, she began running express trains on the former Great Western route from Paddington, here, in 1948. A four-cylinder Castle 4-6-0 could match her, while a King was a different proposition altogether. But gas turbines were all the rage with the RAF and airlines. Could a locomotive benefit from the same technology? Perhaps, but 18000 proved to be smoky, noisy and much disliked by chauvinistic Western Region crews. Even painting her in GW Brunswick green failed to do the trick.

← Bulleid's Leader 0-6-6-0 of 1949 was a fine idea. The BR Southern Region locomotive should have been able to match a diesel, with clear views for the crew and 100 per cent of its weight carried on its driving wheels. In practice, Leader was foxed by too many engineering novelties. Her firemen were expected to work in a hellhole of a compartment. On test, the solitary prototype played up no end. Only on the very last day of her trials did she show a glimpse of what she might have been, a modern 1,500hp, 90mph steam engine to outfox diesels.

↑ Fury was indeed furious. Here she is at the Hyde Park Works of the North British Locomotive Company, Glasgow, on February 7, 1930, looking fit to burst. Which she did, killing her crew. Fury, a high-pressure compound based on the frames of an LMS Royal Scot 4-6-0, was a collaboration between North British and the LMS. Her Schmidt boiler sent steam at 900psi to a single inside cylinder, exhausting it at 250psi through outside cylinders. Bang. That might have been the end of Fury, but she was rebuilt as British Legion, precursor of an improved breed of Royal Scots, in 1935.

This is the monorail at the New York World's Fair, 1964–5. A World's Fair, or Expo, was never the same without one. The futuristic Wuppertal overhead railway had been much published, while monorails were the stuff of Marvel and DC comics in the US, of Dan Dare, Space Pilot of the Future in *The Eagle* comic published in London from 1950. Monorails had a touch of Jules Vernes, H G Wells and the Space Race about them. They were also a practical means of transport at big public events like this since they kept the ground clear of vehicles, which have never mixed too well with milling crowds. Fifty-one million people visited the 1964–5 New York World's Fair; this was a disappointment to the organisers, who expected 70 million. They came to gawp at displays in 175 pavilions spread across 643 acres at a total cost of about $1 billion. The fair was managed by 70-year-old Robert Moses, who had led the American people to the 1939–40 New York World's Fair. They would have been chuffed to witness these sleek monorail cars, harbingers of a future where nuclear electricity would be "too cheap to meter", and trains ran in the sky.

Seven two-car monorail units offered visitors an eight-minute ride around the World's Fair in "air-conditioned comfort". The future was always going to be air-conditioned, with huge nuclear power stations making it possible for everyone to live in an arctic breeze, even in Manhattan, at the height of the summer. This image captures the bright and breezy, breakfast-cereal-packet-meets-Walt-Disney style of the fair. One of the most popular rides, aside from the monorail, was "Small World", a tribute to the work of Unicef sponsored by Pepsi-Cola. Delighted children and bewildered adults were taken on a theme-park ride on little guided boats where they got to meet happy, smiling automata children singing "It's a Small World", over and over again. Were the designers high as kites when they worked on this? Probably not, but then this was the 1960s. "Small World" was moved to Disneyland in California. The monorail vanished. It had run through a vision of the future when concerns for ecology meant pretty much nothing to anyone. If you dropped off at the Du Pont pavilion, for example, you could enjoy the corporation's clap-happy musical, *Wonderful World of Chemistry*, featuring such appropriate numbers as "The Happy Plastic Family."

↑   A mean-looking train of the future that was so very nearly a reality. This is British Rail's four-car APT-E (Advanced Passenger Train – Experimental). It was planned in 1969 and began running, after a run-in with the engine drivers' trade union ASLEF, in 1972. Equipped with four 300hp Leyland 350 gas turbines powering two GEC nose-suspended traction motors, this revolutionary tilting train was soon speeding along at more than 150mph. BR engineers decided, perhaps once and for all, that gas turbines were not suited to the UK's rapid stop-start services, numerous speed restrictions and frequent signal and permanent way checks. This experiment was

shunted off to the National Railway Museum, York, in 1976. It led, though, to the all-electric APT-P (Advanced Passenger Train – Prototype) of 1974 onwards, which went into temporary main-line service on the Euston–Glasgow service. There were complaints of nausea induced by her ability to tilt through bends, although many BR engineers suspected this was due more to alcohol than the train's nimble exertions. APT-P was withdrawn prematurely, with a catalogue of faults, but not before she had reached 162mph in 1979, and informed the design of the fully tested Italian Pendolino trains that privatized British train companies are now buying.

→   Magnetic levitation as a means for making trains go has been a goal of engineers and scientists for seventy years or more. At the end of the twentieth century, the dream became a reality. This is Japan Central Railway's Maglev test train on its 18.4 km test track near Tsuru City, Yahanashi prefecture, in 1998. On December 2nd, 2003, this train reached 581kph. The remote controlled three-car unit is lifted 10mm above its guide track by powerful magnets and then hurled along, near silently, by series of magnets attracting or opposing one another. German engineers, of Transrapid, had been working on the same idea; at the outset of 2004, they completed

work with the Chinese government and the city of Shanghai on the construction of a regular Maglev train linking central Shanghai with Pudong Airport. The train accelerates to 300kph in two minutes, reaching a top speed of 430kph on the 30km run. A popular attraction for the people of Shanghai, many of those riding this revolutionary train have never flown. Not so far away, QJ class 2-10-2s, built in the 1990s, are still hauling freight trains bringing raw materials to cities like Shanghai to make such ventures possible.

↑ Atomic-powered trains were all the rage in 1955. This was at the height of the Cold War, when nuclear power was on many people's minds. Armageddon seemed just around the corner, which was fine for religious cranks but not for regular human beings and every other creature that just wanted to live. This comic-book train, should it ever have been built, would have been a one-way ride to eternity. Imagine that reactor blowing. The illustration is charming, depicting a kind of Robbie the Robot on rails, but give me a King Arthur or Merchant Navy any day.

↗ This is more like it, a French turbo-train on display at the Paris Air Show, 1973. This is basically an airliner fuselage crowned with a jet turbine promising to whisk passengers from Charles de Gaulle-Roissy airport to Rue du Rivoli in two minutes. Significantly, this whizzy design was on show just before the Oil Crisis of 1973–74 made Europe, and even the United States, think of reducing their careless fuel consumption. It was also during this Paris Air Show that the Soviet Tu-144 supersonic passenger jet crashed. Perhaps it might be a good idea to take a Crampton to Paris instead.

→ And this is even more like it, David Wardale's thoroughly engineered proposal for a new, 200km/h steam locomotive for leisure and enthusiast rail travel. Wardale's 5AT is a serious commercial proposition for a compact 3,500ihp 4-6-0. Its ability to accelerate rapidly and its high top speed would allow it to run on main lines without hindrance. New materials technology would make this different from its predecessors in terms of stresses, strains, reliability and overall efficiency. It will retain the look and sound of a conventional steam locomotive, because that is what 99 per cent of people would choose. Due in 2010.

172

WAR + POLITICS

Where Trevithick, Stephenson and Brunel saw railways and trains as symbols of progress, and as revolutionary contributions to the peaceful workings of local and national economies, politicians seized on their potential for darker purposes. The train could go to war. Its tracks could be spread out from their citadels of power to help conquer other nations. It could move troops and munitions quickly. It could be used to crush uprisings in far-flung colonies (p176). It could be employed to humiliate your enemy (p188). It could help whip up popular support (p194).

The cynicism of politicians had the power to transform the train from a force for good to one of perverted science. The trains that took Jews, and others who fell foul of Adolf Hitler's regime, to Nazi death camps were a hellish low point in railway history. Another was the bombing of commuter trains in Madrid in March 2004 by vicious, godless creeps who got their kicks from killing people in love with life.

The cynicism of politicians who conspired to flog off Britain's main line railways to fast-buck private companies in the late 1990s also beggars belief. A state-owned railway starved of investment for decades, but that on the whole had done its best, was replaced by a lottery of business companies that ran the railways to seed while sucking promiscuously on the dugs of unprecedented government subsidies.

The majority of politicians in Britain and the US had long lost interest in railways. In the age of motorways, jet planes and Star Wars, they had new toys to play with. Margaret Thatcher, the "Iron Lady" of British politics in the 1980s, famously despised trains. Meanwhile, throughout continental Europe, Russia, China and Japan, the train has been taken very seriously indeed. In these countries, investment in efficient railways has been paying off handsomely.

The train is an environmentally sound form of transport compared with airliners, air-freighters, cars and lorries. It may not offer politicians the sheer excitement of the latest military hardware or dotcom business adventure, but it is as important as it has ever been. No sensible twenty-first century politician should adopt the contemporary British MPs' contempt for the train; these dim-witted souls will soon enough be shunted into one of history's sidings as the railways of the future speed on.

Railways have played many memorable roles in political history. Lenin arriving at the Finland Station, St Petersburg, aboard his "sealed train" from Helsinki, bringing the October Revolution in his luggage. The military trains of Adolf Hitler and Marshall Mannerheim, hero of Finland, both fighting Stalin in the 1940s, one to extend his grisly empire, the other for the liberation of his country. The signing of first the German and then the French surrenders in 1914 and 1940 (p182) in the saloon of an Orient Express car at Compiegne. Che Guevara's assault on the Cuban army's armoured train at Santa Clara, 1958, that signalled the collapse of the grim dictatorship of Fulgencio Battista.

There have been moments of momentous geo-political history. The completion of the transcontinental railway across the United States in 1869 (p33). The arrival of the Trans-Siberian railway in Vladivostok in 1914. The launch of the Eurostar service between Paris, Brussels and London in 1994, symbolizing a united Europe.

One man who believed in a common bond between Britain, Europe and the United States was Winston Churchill. When the great man died in 1965, his funeral train was pulled from Waterloo by Battle of Britain Pacific 34051 Winston Churchill. In the story of the railways' fraught relationship with politics and war, this was their finest hour.

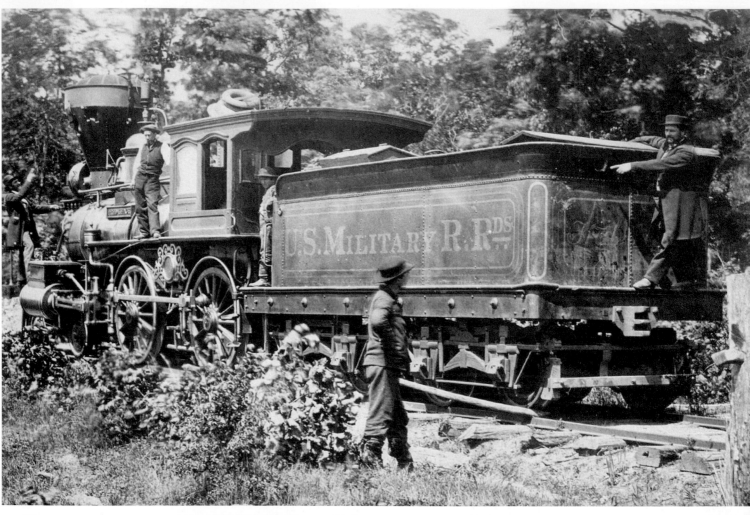

↑ A railroad engineer in the service of the Union Army points to US Military Railroad American-type 4-4-0, Fred Leach, near Inion Mills on the Orange & Alexandria Railroad, August 1, 1863. The locomotive has been gunned through its smokestack and tender by Confederate troops. The American Civil War was the first major conflict reported through photography. It was also the first major war in which the railroad played such a decisive part. The Union Army's reliance on superior communications technology was key to its success. Locomotives purpose-built for war service in the 20th century were, quite sensibly, never so elaborately decorated as the highly wrought Fred Leach.

↗ Another Civil War photograph by the indefatigable Andrew J Russell, Virginia, 1862. Here US Military Railroad personnel attempt to right an overturned American-type 4-4-0, derailed on the Manassas Gap Railroad by Confederate troops. The US Civil War was a brutal affair, setting brother against brother, yet in terms of the future US and world economy, it introduced the idea of mass production: guns, uniforms and locomotives were made to common designs with interchangeable parts rather than custom made in craft tradition as they had been before. Something like 25,000 American-type 4-4-0s, with their familiar giant smokestacks, cowcatchers and elaborate cabs, were to run on US

railroads, playing their part, in war and peace, in opening up North America to settlers and knitting the United States together.

→ Here the US Military Railroad Construction Corps are busy at work – except for the foremen hiding behind their statutory beards – making repairs to a section of the Orange & Alexandria Railroad, Virginia. This line was used by both Union and Confederate armies to supply troops: it was hotly contested and frequently damaged. The crew are taking a rest on the footplate of their 4-4-0. The fireman has been feeding the locomotive's grate with logs. Far less efficient than coal, these were easy to obtain, especially in wartime; they also explain the billowing profile of the giant smokestacks of these early US locomotives. These acted as spark-arrestors; there was enough fire in the Civil War from

both sides without locomotives adding their dollar's worth.

WAR + POLITICS 175

Picture Post, September 9

↑　British soldiers in pith helmets and bush-ranger hats leave for the front in what looks to be a rather comfortable and well-ventilated train during the Boer War (1899–1902). This conflict pitted the might of the British Empire, fielding half a million troops, against 88,000 sharpshooting Boer settlers in the two Afrikaner republics, the Orange Free State and the South African Republic. The crowd on the platform here at Cape Town in November 1899 is in holiday mood, dressed in summer clothes, a sea of hats, and waving the Union Flag. Scenes like this were to be repeated, and recorded by photographers, over the next half-century as the railways played an

ever increasing and important role in moving troops and munitions from home fronts to front lines. Trains were a vital ingredient to the success of Lord Kitchener's and Earl Robert's armies, enabling British troops to relieve the besieged towns of Kimberly, Ladysmith and Mafeking. When generals Christian Rudolf de Wet and Jacobus Hercules De la Rey attacked British railway lines, Kitchener responded by protecting them with barbed wire and blockhouses. Along the railways he set up concentration camps, a British invention, that caused the death of 20,000 Boer women and children.

→　US Soldiers of the 17th Infantry head to the front during the Philippine Insurrection, or more properly, the US–Philippine War of 1899–1902. It looks to be a considerably less comfortable affair than the train taking British troops to fight the Boers, but railways were much less sophisticated in the Philippines. This is also how the Americans saw Filipinos, as underdogs who needed a good kicking when they dared to rise up against their US imperial masters. Many Americans refused to believe that Filipinos were Christians, even though they had experienced 300 years of Spanish rule. These big boy scouts, armed to the teeth, will soon put paid to the

insurrection. The US had annexed the Philippines by force, although President William McKinley preferred to call American action "benevolent assimilation". Filipinos fought a guerrilla war until 1914, but were effectively crushed by 1902. Torture, massacres and concentration camps were some of the methods used to destroy the "niggers", as US troops described the poorly armed Filipinos. It all reminded Fred D Sweet in the Utah Light Infantry of "shooting jack rabbits in Utah, only the rabbits sometimes got away, but the insurgents all died." No wonder these boys are smiling.

↑ The First World War was one of the greatest killing machines yet invented. Millions of young men were minced up on the Western Front, in France and Belgium, between 1914 and 1918. Here two of them, young British Tommies, board their train to the Kent coast from Victoria station, on a rainy morning in London, December 1914. One carries a Lee Enfield rifle over his shoulder; both carry brown paper parcels wrapped up in string. Are they travelling First Class? They certainly deserve it. By this time, the train enabled the rapid deployment of troops not just at home, but also towards the front line in Europe. Many British locomotives— notably Great Central Railway Robinson 2-8-0s, and Great Western Dean Goods 0-6-0s – went to war, too.

↗ September 27, 1918. Australian troops board trains for operations in "black areas". You would have thought that there was enough killing for every full-blooded white Australian in the mud, trenches and beaches of France, Belgium and Gallipoli; the First World War still had six weeks to run its course. But, no. Here, Australian troops set off by train to cull feisty Aboriginals somewhere in the Outback. It was good target practice. Between 1788 and 1921, the Aboriginal population of Australia fell from approximately 300,000 to 60,000; at least 20,000 were shot for the loss of some 2,500 whites. Between 1800 and 1877, the entire Aboriginal population of Tasmania was wiped out. During the Second World War, Australian Aboriginals were to fight Axis powers alongside white troops.

→ It's 1914. German troops in spiked helmets wave from the window of a Third Class carriage on their way to be slaughtered on the Western Front. It is odd to see these images repeated time and again across the world. Jingoistic young men, sold into war by vicious older men, smile and wave for cameras, families and sweethearts from trains, only to return on other trains on stretchers. It is said that every German family lost at least one of its members during the First World War. Still, at least these young bloods will get to the front efficiently. Many of the railways of Germany, unified under Bismarck, the "Iron Chancellor", in 1871, were run on military lines, the Prussian State Railways in particular.

↑ Hospital trains played an important part in the First World War, not only in Europe, but in the US and Canada, too, where trains like this were increasingly on hand to transport wounded soldiers home after they disembarked from their voyage across the Atlantic. This car, where the doctor in charge is turned towards the camera, is equipped with beds, fans, blinds, telephone, typewriter and, ah yes, a spittoon. When Britain and France went to war in 1914, it was quickly realized that hospital trains would be needed. The first, built by the French, were nothing more than goods wagons hastily converted to carry the wounded without heating, proper suspension or corridor connections. These were soon replaced by 16-coach hospital trains built in France and Britain.

↗ The armoured train made its debut in August 1914, pioneered by the Austro-Hungarian army. A standard version, PzZug I-VIII, was built by MAV in Budapest from 1915. Here one of these armoured trains — viewed as an alternative to the tank, although rather less able to move freely — is got under steam towards the end of the war in 1918. The armoured wagons house 80mm cannons that are able to fire forwards as well as to either side. The locomotive, despite its fearsome appearance, is nothing more than a 377 class 0-6-0 tank, with outside Stephenson valve gear, a standard Austro-Hungarian branch-line and shunting engine of the 1890s. Nine of these trains were built, five serving until the end of hostilities. They were considered to be a great success.

→ French soldiers being carried off a hospital train, Rheims, September 1914. War had by now become something like an industrial process. The mass production of guns, ammunition, poison gas and equipment had all been made possible by the invention of the locomotive-hauled train. Trains carried raw materials to factories to make the machinery of death. They carried the machinery of death to front lines. They carried soldiers to the front. They carried them back again minus limbs and minds. Men like Richard Trevithick (p28), so enthused with the notion of scientific progress, would never have expected his invention to be turned into an aid to mass killing.

← November 11, 1918. The Armistice ending the First World War has just been signed inside carriage 2419 of the Orient Express at Compiegne. The victorious French General Foch poses with French and British military attachés. The carriage was then moved by the French Army to a museum in Paris, where it rested for the next 22 years. The following year the Treaty of Versailles demanded punitive, humiliating and, ultimately, unrealistic war reparations against the new German Weimar Republic. The groundswell of popular feeling in Germany against the treaty was a key factor in the rise of Adolf Hitler.

↑ As if through a glass darkly, a Waffen-SS trooper peers into the saloon of Orient Express carriage 2419, June 21, 1940. Adolf Hitler is seen contemplating his conquest of France and the signing of the French surrender the following day. Hitler insisted that the very same carriage in which the 1918 armistice had been signed was brought from Paris to Compiegne, to humiliate the French. To add to the topsy-turvy story of these Orient Express carriages, in 1918 the Bolshevik government of Rolls-Royce owner, V I Lenin, took 161 of them captive for use, presumably by the aristocracy of labour.

Overleaf left →→ November 11, 1919. A year after the armistice ending the First World War had been signed, passengers and staff of the Great Western Railway at Paddington stand to attention, hats in hand, to observe a two-minute silence for those who had fallen in the conflict. This was the year in which an even greater number of people than had died in the war were killed by an influenza virus that swept the world. The railways, meanwhile, got steadily back into their stride, although they would be faced with their own war with rival traffic by road, if not yet seriously by air.

Overleaf right →→ During the Second World War, London was heavily bombed. The "Phoney War", where nothing seemed to happen at home during the Battle of France, gave way to the Blitz of 1940–41. This scene of grim destruction (1940) is William Barlow's magnificent train shed at St Pancras station, built as the London terminus of the Midland Railway. In 1923, Britain's many main line railways were grouped into the Big Four: one of these was the London Midland and Scottish (LMS), known to its detractors as "'ell of a mess", which it was here, but through no fault of its own.

↑ London school children, gas masks in boxes worn over their shoulders, evacuate London by train in June 1940. Over the next weeks, Hitler attempted to destroy the Royal Air Force before launching Operation Seelowe (Sea Lion), the invasion of England. The RAF's "few" to whom so much was owed, in Spitfires and Hurricanes, just managed to destroy the confidence of the Luftwaffe. A part of the German failure was the decision by Hitler and Göring to bomb London to destroy civilian morale instead of concentrating their air force against all but exhausted military targets. These children were sent away just in time. Their evacuation was organized by Frank Pick, visionary

chief executive of the London Passenger Transport Board. Many, though, missed London and, despite the bombs, returned home.

↗ Kilted non-commissioned officers of a Scottish regiment prepare to go to war with Nazi Germany. Who knows what the crisply uniformed Wehrmacht troops made of these lads, who would have fought with courage and ferocity. Here, they set out on the long journey to London, at a time when trains were becoming increasingly heavy. A Gresley A4 streamlined Pacific – one might well be at the head of this train – designed to run seven- to nine-car trains of up to 235 tons at high speed between Edinburgh, Newcastle and London, would be expected to haul troop trains like this of up to 20 and more coaches weighing 750 to 800 tons. They, too, proved fine fighters for Britain during the six-year war.

→ This is Compiegne , on September 17, 1942. By this time, France was divided into two zones: the north under direct German rule, and the south, Vichy France, under the puppet regime of General Petain. These wounded French so, despite the bombs, ldiers are arriving back home; the condition of their release is that for every three wounded soldiers returned from Germany, one able-bodied man would make the return journey. The train is decorated with garlands of flowers, and these soldiers are undoubtedly pleased to be going back to their families. It will be nearly another two years, though, before the SNCF was back in service with a liberated France. Oddly, many of the towns you pass

through along the Cote d'Azur are still extreme right-wing strongholds.

← Brief Encounter. Here is evidence of a tragic love affair between Adolf Hitler (1889–1945) and Benito Mussolini (1883–1945). The date is September 1937, and the Italian Duce is making his fond farewell from his special train at Berlin Zoo station. Stupidly, Mussolini allowed himself to he drawn into Hitler's war. All it gained him was the sack of Italy and his own ignominious end, strung upside down from a lamp post with his mistress by Italian partisans. Mussolini, like Hitler, was keen on trains. So much so that on his famous "march on Rome" in 1922, at the end of which he was proclaimed prime minister by King Vittorio Emmanuele, Mussolini went by train. Others marched. It was also said of him that whatever else he did, or failed to do, at least he "made the trains run on time". This particular visit was wittily satirized by Charlie Chaplin in his film *Modern Times*, in which the red carpet drawn up for the Mussolini-style dictator is always in the wrong place as his Hitler-style leader tries to order his guest's train to stop in the right place. Neither of these morally cretinous leaders knew when to stop; hence their downfall.

↓ Adolf Hitler and Joachim von Ribbentrop, sitting beside the Führer's armoured train during the invasion of Poland, September 1939. This vast military machine made frequent overnight journeys between Berlin, Hitler's seat of government, and the Wolfschanze (Wolf's Lair), his forward command headquarters in the Silesian Forest, East Prussia. Originally called Amerika, it was renamed Brandenburg when the United States entered the Second World War in 1941; unwisely, Hitler had declared war on Uncle Sam. His train was equipped with 20mm anti-aircraft guns, meeting rooms, a restaurant, private suites and troop quarters; it was so heavy that it demanded the services of two locomotives. Those who worked in the train complained that it was claustrophobic. Hitler was impressed by all forms of powerful machinery, notably Mercedes-Benz tourers and powerful locomotives. It was a great satisfaction to him that, in 1936, the year his troops re-entered the Rhineland, the Deutsche Reichsbahn 4-6-4 05 002 captured the world speed record for steam. He had an extraordinary knowledge of technical and engineering details. Luckily, his judgement as a military leader proved to be deeply flawed when he launched Operation Barbarossa, the invasion of the Soviet Union, in June 1941. Brandenburg was never to arrive in Moscow.

Who do you think you are kidding, Mr Hitler? Gallant members of the Home Guard ("Dads' Army") and regular army troops man the Romney Hythe and Dymchurch Railway's miniature armoured train – the only one of its kind – at New Romney, Kent, during the Battle of Britain, 1940. The train comprised Hercules, an 8.25-ton, 15-inch gauge 4-8-2 designed by Henry Greenly and built by Davey Paxman in 1927, and two bogie wagons from the Ravenglass and Eskdale Railway, Cumbria, converted into mobile platforms with two Lewis guns and a Boyes anti-tank rifle. The RHDR ran for 13½ miles along the Kent coast, flanked by the Romney Marshes. This is where Hitler was expected to have invaded England.

Advertisement for the naming ceremony of Southern Railway "Battle of Britain" Pacific 21C51 615 Squadron, Guildford station, October 1948. The RAF's 615 "County of Surrey" Squadron flew Hawker Hurricanes during the Battle of Britain from several airfields within the embrace of the Southern Railway. It went on to fly the first Spitfires in India and Burma against the Japanese in 1943. Oliver Bulleid's Battle of Britain Pacifics were strong, if slippery, machines. Weighing just 86 tons, they could negotiate cross-country as well as main lines. During the locomotive trials conducted that year by the new, state-owned British Railways, BBs showed they could tackle any British railway with mastery. They had a charismatic look, could exert 2,400ihp and exceed 100mph. Spitfires and Hurricanes would have approved.

The scene is Debert, Nova Scotia, 1942. Canadian railways have brought a train load of Sherman tanks to be shipped to Europe, while a tri-motor transport plane flies overhead. The sheer productivity of North American industry was to spell the end of German military power on the Western Front. Hitler, who rarely travelled abroad, had been unable to gauge the scale of the North American response, first Canada and then the United States, to his aggression. North American industry was able to produce arms, aircraft and equipment in prodigious quantities. The 35-ton Sherman was the US army's main battle tank throughout the Second World War; what these 49,000 tanks lacked in armour-plate and firepower, they made up in simplicity and reliability, like freight locomotive 2425.

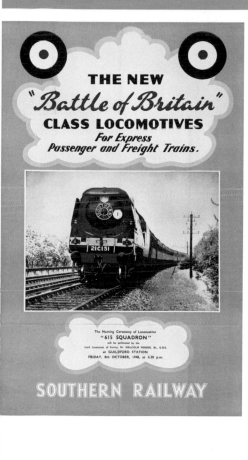

THE NEW
"Battle of Britain"
CLASS LOCOMOTIVES
*For Express
Passenger and Freight Trains.*

The Naming Ceremony of Locomotive
"615 SQUADRON"
will be performed by the
Lord Lieutenant of Surrey, Sir MALCOLM FRASER, Bt., O.B.E.
at GUILDFORD STATION
FRIDAY, 8th OCTOBER, 1948, at 4.30 p.m.

SOUTHERN RAILWAY

↑   This remarkable photograph, dated January 15, 1945, shows German prisoners of war travelling to a prison camp on board a US train departing Boston, Massachusetts. The US was keen to extract information from captured expert German soldiers, engineers, designers and scientists. The rocket scientist Werner von Braun, who designed the V2 rocket that caused death and destruction in England in the last months of the war, was one such prisoner of war; von Braun was to become NASA's chief rocket scientist, and made the Moon landings of 1969 possible. His former employer, Adolf Hitler, had dreamed only of conquering the world; he was too old-fashioned to have thought of invading the heavens. For these Wermacht soldiers, doubtless many skilled specialists among them, the war is over. They look relaxed and comfortable aboard a classic American open-plan carriage, luggage neatly stowed, and two equally relaxed GIs keeping an eye on them. The US was, in fact, quite unprepared for the sheer number of POWs it would hold during the war: a total of 425,000, of whom 371,000 were German, and 51,000 Italian, housed in camps mainly in the remote south-west, well away from US industry. Nazis were imprisoned separately.

→   One of the most infamous use of trains ever was to transport millions of Jews to their deaths in concentration camps in Germany and Poland. These were situated mostly in remote rural areas reached by branch lines. Here, though, a train load of Jews being transferred from Buchenwald to another death camp further away from advancing Allied armies in 1945 is rescued by Czech partisans. They had been travelling in open-topped wagons – probably drawn by one of the 6,000-plus brutally functional Kriegslok 2-10-0s, built throughout occupied Europe – and for three weeks without food and water, according to their liberators. It goes without saying that many died along the way. It was not only Jews who travelled in this beastly manner: Soviet POWs, Communists, gypsies, homosexuals, the physically and mentally disabled, Jehovah's Witnesses, Social Democrats, partisans and Polish intellectuals were among fellow passengers. Between May 14 and June 8, 1944, a total of 437,402 Hungarian Jews were transported to Auschwitz on 48 trains, probably the largest mass transportation of the war. The German railways, ever efficient, kept exact records. Even as Nazi Germany collapsed, the SS continued its transportation of Jews in the hope of eliminating them before the Allied victory.

↑ August, 1943, Quebec, Ontario. President Franklin Delano Roosevelt rides in style from Montreal to a wartime conference in Ottowa. His locomotive is one of the five members of the Canadian National U4-a class streamlined 4-8-4. With 24 x 30-inch cylinders and a boiler pressure of 275psi, this is a powerful machine, and a good choice for one of the best presidents the US has ever had. The U4-a class, tested in wind tunnels, was built in 1936 by the Montreal Locomotive Works, and ran until 1960. One is preserved at the National Museum of Science and Industry, Montreal.

↗ Here comes George Bush Jr, with the light of Jesus in his eyes, and Dick Cheney, ready to smoke 'em out, whoever and wherever the bad guys are. This scene at Oxnard, California, is from a whistle-stop tour during the controversial election campaign of 2000. Baby Bush was following in a long tradition of US presidential hopefuls by hectoring the electorate from the back of a train. In an age when US passenger traffic is dominated by the car, it was rather touching to see the warring presidential candidate out and about by old-fashioned train.

→ July 5, 1952, Hastings, Nebraska. Presidential candidate General Dwight D Eisenhower speaks from the back of a train, between huge loudspeakers, bristling microphones and Mrs Eisenhower's flowers, during a whistle-stop tour of Nebraska as that year's Republican Convention got under way. Eisenhower had been the Allied commander-in-chief of Operation Overlord – the invasion of German-occupied Europe – during the Second World War, but unlike certain future US presidents, he never wore a military uniform in civilian life, nor landed on an aircraft-carrier trying to look like Tom Cruise. Eisenhower was a real hero; a train was good enough for him.

→→ September 8, 1960, Richmond, California. Democrat presidential hopeful John F Kennedy stares out the swirling floral carpet of his campaign train during a break from speaking during a two-day railroad tour of the Sunshine State. Even then, the photographer is still in action. Kennedy, who beat Richard Nixon to the presidency in the 1960 elections, was to be assassinated by Lee Harvey Oswald during a tour of Dallas, Texas, in November 1963, riding in a 1961 Lincoln Continental open tourer. His presidency was to be characterized by great style; his sojourn at the White House was described as a new Camelot.

← US President Abraham Lincoln was assassinated on April 15, 1865, the day he was due to take a test ride aboard the United States, a lavish Pullman Car custom-made for this victor of the Civil War. The first journey he made in the United States was as a corpse in an open coffin. The President's funeral train travelled 1,654 miles from Washington DC to Springfield, Illinois, along a complex route that more or less followed Lincoln's election trail of 1861, with a detour to Chicago; it took more than two weeks so that as many Americans as possible could see the late President and his train. Here, the Cleveland, Columbus & Cincinatti Railroad 4-4-0 locomotive Nashville is

prepared at Cleveland before taking the train on the funeral march – it was certainly no run – to Columbus. The locomotive is lavishly decorated with bunting, drapes, black-fringed presidential flags and a portrait of Lincoln above its cowcatcher. Some 20 different locomotives took part in this stately procession; millions of people witnessed its passing, or came to see the nine-car train at stations. Sadly, the United States, the first Pullman Car many Americans would have seen, was destroyed by fire in 1911.

↑ Pallbearers carry the draped coffin of King George VI from his funeral train at King's Cross station, London, February 12, 1952. George VI has been king and emperor during the Second World War; a shy chap with a pronounced stammer, he was a model of a good king and family man. The three women, draped in black, to the right of the picture are: Queen Mary, King George's mother; Queen Elizabeth, his wife; and Queen Elizabeth II, his eldest daughter. The train has come from Wolferton, nearest station to Sandringham, Norfolk, where the royal family has one of its homes. It comprises varnished teak LNER coaches, with the King's hearse painted black with a

white roof. B17 4-6-0 Sandringham pulled the train from Wolferton to King's Lynn, and the new British Railways' Pacific 70000 Britannia on to King's Cross. After lying in state, the coffin was taken to Windsor Castle; this train was to have been headed by Great Western 4-6-0 Windsor Castle, which had borne George V's coffin in 1936, but as this was being overhauled, nameplates were swapped with those of 7013 Bristol Castle, built in 1948, the year that Prince Charles, current heir to the throne, was born.

198 ADVERTISING

I interviewed Terence Cuneo shortly before this distinguished railway artist died. Cuneo was never taken seriously by the art establishment, but that was its loss. He was a good painter, but his subject was, first and foremost, the steam locomotive. This, unless by Turner or Cezanne, has only ever been thin gruel for directors of galleries who prefer to invest in such improving subjects, or installations, as smelly unmade beds, pickled sheep, heads sculpted in the artist's blood... anything, in fact, rather than a depiction of a train. Trains have always been too, too common (my dears) for serious art galleries.

Cuneo had no worries. He was commissioned not just by wealthy railway enthusiasts, but also by the railways themselves. He was master of the public information poster at a time – the 1950s and early 1960s – when railways still thought it their duty to inform passengers of the progress they were making and of the tasks they performed for their benefit. Only much later would they adopt the tactics of advertising agencies promoting the virtues of baked beans and breakfast cereals.

I suppose this was because the railways seemed like a given at the time. They were a public service that existed to get goods and people to the most remote destinations, to villages all but impossible to reach safely, or in anything like good time, by road.

This sense of public service is far from dead. The Swiss run their railways to precise, clockwork schedules; when roads are blocked by snow or made treacherous by ice and fog, and planes are unable to fly, Swiss trains will always get through. Significantly, perhaps, it was the Swiss who set many of the high standards of typography, poster design and advertising that have characterized their railways.

In countries like Russia, there was never much need to advertise the railways. How else was a largely carless and poor population going to travel across Siberia when they needed to, or were compelled to at the point of a bayonet? Even today, if you study a map of Siberia, you will find remarkably few roads. Remote, blasted by savage winter weather and with precious little traffic, they would be expensive luxuries, made irrelevant by the general efficiency of existing and new railways.

Perhaps because railway advertising has rarely been about a hard sell, it has often used whimsy, romance and wit to promote its services rather than the crude, supermarket "prices slashed, we're practically giving it away" style of today's clownish "no-frills" airlines. Railways have always been more dignified than such pile-them-high, sell-them-cheap enterprises that have nothing to offer but bargain basement prices. Their point, I suppose, is that no one cares any more about how they travel, except for silly celebrities who like to pay for First Class airline tickets to show they have made it; all most people care about is getting to their destination cheaply and quickly. And that is indeed all anyone cares about squeezed aboard a noisy jet with signs imploring "please remove your legs if you wish to sit here".

There have been some notorious lapses of taste in railway advertising, as there always will be in any form of advertising, publishing or broadcasting when railways, newspapers and television channels try to "get down with the kids". Such tactics are as cringe-making as they are dumbly patronising. Try the British Rail advert of the 1970s in which the Swedish pop group Abba ask youngsters to keep their stations clean (p212). The best railway adverts, some of which you can see here, simply make you want to travel. In true style.

STRASSBURGER STRASSENBAHNEN

WINTER-FAHRPLAN 1898 99.
Trambahnen

FAHRPLAN

CHEMINS DE FER DE L'OUEST ET DE BRIGHTON

PARIS À LONDRES
PAR ROUEN, DIEPPE
& NEWHAVEN
DÉPARTS TOUS LES JOURS
DE LA GARE St LAZARE
à 10ʰ 20 matin et 9ʰ 20 soir
PRIX DES BILLETS

BILLETS SIMPLES			BILLETS D'ALLER & RETOUR		
1ʳᵉ classe	2ᵉ classe	3ᵉ classe	1ʳᵉ classe	2ᵉ classe	3ᵉ classe
48ᶠ25	35ᶠ	23ᶠ25	82ᶠ75	58ᶠ75	41ᶠ50

MAURICE TOUSSAINT LONDRES 37

CORNILLE - Imprimeur

← ← Early railway advertising was a jumble of typefaces, type sizes and timetables. This one, dating from summer 1857, announces twice daily through trains from Montreal to New York, 390 miles, via the Rutland and Burlington Railway. It is justly proud of the fact that this is the only service connecting the Canadian and US cities that can get passengers to their destination the same day, at an average speed of a little less than 25mph. The train itself, composed of eight-wheeled bogie cars headed by a classic, mid-century American 4-4-0, is barely celebrated in a tiny, and slightly unrealistic, engraving.

← A truly historic Union Pacific advert, from May 10, 1869, announcing the grand opening of through services across the US from east to west coasts. A giant stag blocks the view of the tiny train itself smoking its way across the continent, but the selling points for train travel are loud and clear: a promise of gold and silver at the end of the line; dining and Pullman cars; a health-giving ride across the Rocky Mountains; safer than sea travel. And, Omaha to San Francisco in just four days? What else could any God- and Indian-fearing traveller want?

↖ Strassburger Strassenbahnen timetable for winter 1898–99, or "Do you think, *mein liebling*, that we should with such a low class crowd be travelling?" The elegant fräulein in the red outfit looks concerned. But this is the 19th century, dammit, and the train – a steam tram, in fact – may well offer three classes of accommodation to keep the aristocracy, bourgeoisie and proletariat separate. Strasbourg was in German hands at the time, the Alsace being annexed by Prussia after its victory in the war of 1870 with France; it returned to France after German defeat in the First World War.

↑ A lovely ad from 1907, by Maurice Toussaint, a prolific French artist, for the Chemin de Fer de L'Ouest. Come to London every day via Rouen, Dieppe and Newhaven and see the famous guards; except that the guards on duty, bagpipes wailing, outside the Houses of Parliament and Westminster Abbey appear to have escaped, with no change of dress, from the Edinburgh military tattoo. Still, at those fares, *mon braves*, exactly who is complaining? Trains, at this time, were still rarely considered interesting or glamorous enough in their own right to appear in railway advertising; images of destinations predominated.

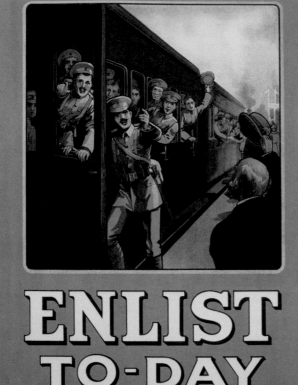

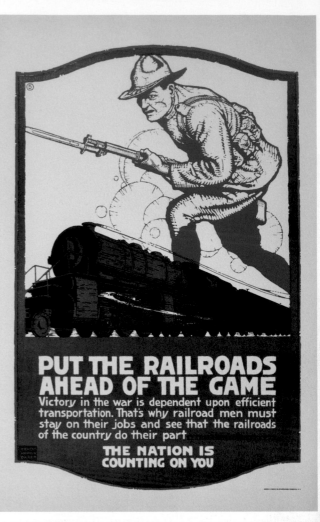

↑ Things must be pretty desperate on the Western Front for a crowd of eager-faced, train-bound Tommies to call on a grandfather to join them in the carnage. A routine British poster, in fact, from the early days of the First World War, to be sung to these words: "Brother Bertie went away to do his bit the other day/ With a smile on his lips and his lieutenant pips upon his shoulder bright and gay/As the train moved out, he said 'Remember me to all the girls'/And then he wagged his paw and went away to war shouting out these pathetic words/'Good-bye-ee, good-bye-ee, wipe the tears, baby dear, from your eye-ee/Though it's hard to part, I know, I'll be tickled to death to go."

↗ The nation is counting on you. It must have been good to be a railwayman in the First World War. Here, a US government poster, designed by Ernest Hamlin Baker (1889–1975), tells railway workers to stick with their jobs rather than to put on a boy-scout hat, pick up a rifle and get killed defending old Europe. Good, too, to have been at the throttle of the fast freight train headed by an early Mallet depicted in the ad, rather than at the end of a German, Austro-Hungarian or Turkish bayonet. The clever thing about the design is the way in which Baker equates the tough, charging soldier with the equally tough, charging train, yet even so, the soldier is given due and proper prominence.

→ Peacetime again, yet there is something deeply stirring, almost warlike, about this 1923 poster by William Hamden Foster depicting the east- and west-bound *Twentieth Century Limited* passing in the night half-way between Chicago and New York. It is a terrific, wintry image designed to instil in potential passengers, especially those considering the rival *Broadway Limited* operated by the Pennsylvania Railroad, the idea of a furiously fast, yet luxurious and reliable, train that rushes through ice, snow, dark and storm while they dine well and sleep soundly in warmly lit Pullman cars. The racing locomotive is one of the late batches of New York Central Pacifics, developed from 1910, that handled this famous train until their replacements by mighty Paul Kiefer-designed Hudsons in 1927.

AS THE "CENTURIES" PASS IN THE NIGHT

The Twentieth Century Limited
of the NEW YORK CENTRAL LINES

NEW YORK CENTRAL R.R CO.

William Thomson Foster
1925

The 20th Century Limited speeding through the Heart of Industrial America

NEW YORK CENTRAL SYSTEM

CROSS AUSTRALIA BY TRANS-AUSTRALIAN RAILWAY

DSB
THE DANISH STATE RAILWAYS

L'ARMENIE SOVIETIQUE

← Steam, streamlining, speed, power and industry: this stirring image, designed by Leslie Ragan (1897–1972) in 1940, depicts the New York Central's peerless *Twentieth Century Limited* racing past US industrial muscle as Europe plunges into war again. It captures, quite beautifully, the way in which the famous train, by now a masterpiece on rails streamlined by Henry Dreyfuss, was itself a fruit of heavy industry. It suggests, too, and quite rightly, that the speeding locomotive is powerful as well as quick; Paul Kiefer's J3-a Hudsons, of which 10 like this were styled especially for the *Twentieth Century Limited* in 1938, could produce 4,725hp.

↖ A powerful poster, by Gert Sellheim (1901–70), from 1935, advertising the Trans-Australian Railway. By this time, the railway locomotive was used widely as a symbol of speed, strength and determined energy. More important, graphic design, influenced by the Bauhaus, had cleaned up its act; posters of the 1930s are often crisp, clear and memorable. Sellheim had trained as an architect in Berlin, Munich and Graz before emigrating to Australia in 1926. He went on to design the flying kangaroo logo for Qantas. This poster captures the heroic qualities of the Trans-Australian Railway, a formidable achievement by navvies and engineers alike.

↑ Faster than fairies, faster than witches... a superb abstract image of a Danish State Railways' express train speeding into the night. A spectral speedometer encompassing the train shows its rate of progress, nudging 120km/h, a top speed dictated by civil engineers, and management, on many contemporary European main lines. This 1937 design, by Aage Rasmussen, is a perfect example of Bauhaus design in the service of 20th-century railways. It is ultra modern, yet captures the romance of a fast steam train racing, dream-like, into some infinite distance. DSB continues to produce posters of the highest design quality.

↑ At the time this poster was designed, around 1930, many western European intellectuals were blindly in love with the notion of Stalin's Soviet Union. They imagined it to be something like this scene, depicting Soviet Armenia, where happy, smiling people lived in beautiful surroundings, where foreigners could tour happily in elegant cars, and trains ran, for the good of all, like clockwork to all parts of the heroic Communist empire. Even so, this poster for Intourist, the Soviet travel agency, is a fine example of 1930s design, and would encourage any keen train traveller to consider a jaunt to exotic Armenia.

↓ Sentimental poster from the Chesapeake and Ohio Railroad, 1938. When the weather is hot and bothersome, and the thought of travelling long distances is about as appealing as having a tooth pulled, perhaps the idea of air-conditioned comfort on board C&O's latest fleet of luxury trains might just tempt potential travellers away from the porch, and off on a trip by *The George Washington* or *The Sportsman* along the route of the Potomac River. The C&O made great play of its extensive air-conditioned services, introduced from 1933. The railroad was ultimately absorbed into the Chessie System by Amtrak in 1971.

↓ This is Chessie the cat, the C&O's mascot in a poster of 1938. Chessie was originally drawn by Guido Gruenewald, an Austrian artist, and discovered in the pages of the *Herald Tribune* in 1933 by Lionel C Probert, the railroad's vice president, public relations and advertising. Chessie, "America's sleepheart", was hugely popular, featuring in sets of playing cards and calendars franchised by the C&O. She appeared in C&O posters right up until the railroad's merger with the Baltimore and Ohio and West Maryland in 1971. Her name was given to the new Amtrak-owned system. She was one cool cat.

→ Mrs Casey Jones, named after the legendary railroad engineer, goes to war in the service of the Pennsylvania Railroad. Just as thousands of British women had worked on railways during the First World War, now it was the turn of American women. Three of the women illustrated are busy cleaning one of the railroad's long-serving and efficient K4 Pacifics, a type that had gone into service in 1914. This simple, yet effective, poster also announces the number of PRR personnel in the armed forces and the 38 who had died in the ranks of Uncle Sam and for European democracy.

→→ All-American muscle. This 1943 PRR wartime ad, in the same series as "Meet Mrs Casey Jones", explains why the railroads play such a key role in the US war effort. Each soldier going abroad to fight Germany, Italy and Japan requires eight tons of equipment, supplies, food and ammunition. The railroads need to move this weight thousands of times over from sources across the United States. The PRR plays its muscular role and passengers, the poster suggests, must remember that freight trains come first. The scale of US freight trains during wartime had to be seen to be believed.

Meet **MRS.** Casey Jones

CASEY'S gone to war . . . so Mrs. Jones is "working on the railroad!"

She is putting in a big day's work oiling and swabbing down giant engines, cleaning and vacuuming cars, handling baggage, selling tickets, moving through the aisles as a trainman.

In fact, she is doing scores of different jobs on the Pennsylvania Railroad—and doing them well. So the men in the armed forces whom she has replaced can take comfort in the fact she has replaced can take comfort in the fact Mrs. Casey Jones is "carrying on" in fine style.

Since the war began, Pennsylvania Railroad has welcomed thousands of women into its ranks of loyal, busy and able workers. They are taking a real part in the railroad's big two-fold job of moving troops and supplies and serving essential civilian needs during the war emergency.

You will find these women, not merely in expected places, such as offices, telephone exchanges and ticket windows . . . you will find them out where "man-size" jobs have to be done: in the round house, in the shops, in the yards, in the terminals, in the cars.

We feel sure the American public will take pride in the way American womanhood has pitched in to keep the Victory trains rolling!

BUY UNITED STATES
WAR BONDS AND STAMPS

PENNSYLVANIA RAILROAD
Serving the Nation

★ 34,101 in the Armed Forces ★ 58 have given their lives for their country

THIS FIGHTER WEIGHS IN AT

8 TONS

ON OUR SCALES

AS YOU would see him on a scale, he would weigh 180 pounds of bone, muscle and fighting energy—a fine specimen of American manhood. But on the scales of the Army—and the Railroads—his "fighting weight" is . . . 8 tons.

This is why: the equipment, supplies, ammunition, food and other items required for every man going overseas average close to 8 tons. What is more, he needs *a ton a month* of all these things as long as he is over there. Or, just *twice* as much a day as the soldier in World War I.

So, you see, the railroad's job isn't only moving troops —but all they require, too. Therefore, if you should find travel not all that it used to be, the Pennsylvania Railroad asks you kindly to remember the above facts. We are doing our best to serve you. But military needs must come first, as all Americans would have it.

BUY UNITED STATES WAR BONDS AND STAMPS

Pennsylvania Railroad
Serving the Nation

★ 41,500 in the Armed Forces ★ 59 have given their lives for their country

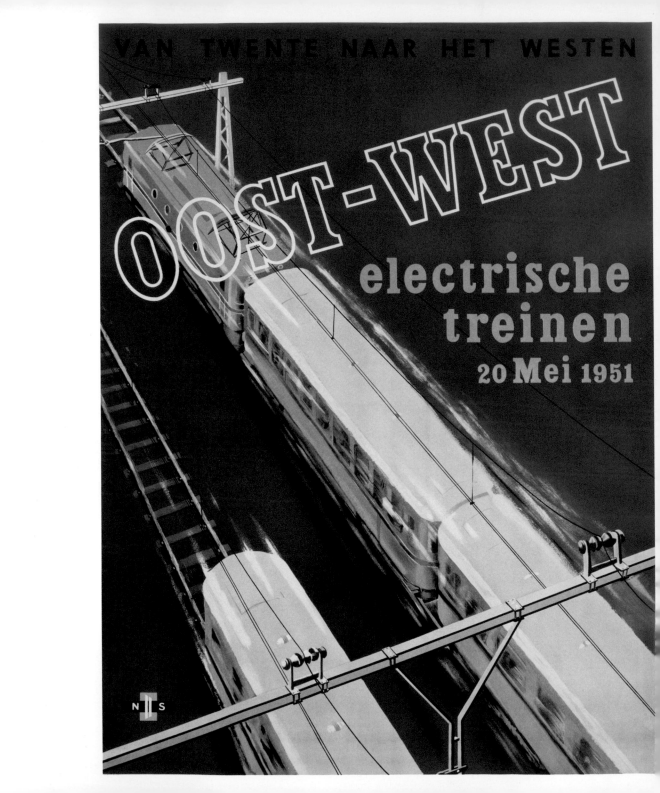

LOCOMOTIVE QUADRICOURANT CC 40100

TRANS EUROP EXPRESS
PARIS - BRUXELLES - AMSTERDAM

CHEMINS DE FER FRANÇAIS

SUMMER ON THE FRENCH RIVIERA
BY THE BLUE TRAIN

Overleaf left ←← In post-war Europe, the pace on the railways was to be made by electric traction. This design from 1951, by Dehaan, celebrates the introduction of electric passenger trains across the Netherlands. The image of speed is heightened by the words "Oost-West" slashing diagonally, and energetically, up and across the poster. The Nederland Spoorwegen electrified at 1,500v and locomotives were variations on French prototypes. The one here is stylized, but is presumably based on the 1100-series BBs newly delivered to the NS.

Overleaf middle ←← The epitome of modern electric power, an SNCF CC40100 locomotive is seen streaking along at the head of a Trans European Express from Paris to Amsterdam when brand new in 1964. This poster by Albert Brenet (born 1903), official artist to the French navy and air force, depicts a moment when European railways, led by the French, were redefining their image and doing their bit to nurture a European community. The CC40100 series were surplanted by TGVs in 1996.

Overleaf right ←← The luxurious Le Train Bleu began service from Calais to the Cote d'Azur in 1922. It was one of the famous blue and gold sleeping trains of La Compagnie des Wagons-Lits that revolutionized continental travel from 1883 when the Belgian entrepreneur, George Nagelmacker, launched his first train, the Orient Express. A hotel-on-wheels, the Blue Train was not particularly fast. In 1930, Captain Woolf Barnato, chairman of Bentley Motors, raced the train from Cannes to Calais, in a fastback 6.5-litre Bentley. Crossing the Channel, Barnato and the Bentley were in London four minutes before Le Train Bleu steamed, comfortably, into Calais.

↓ Oh brave new world that hath such stations in it.... There is something truly naïve about this cartoon-like 1960 BR poster announcing the future completion of the new Manchester Piccadilly station. The architecture is a poor pastiche of a generic contemporary European office block and the upswept concrete concourse of Rome Termini. But as this was the starting point of a new generation of 100mph BR electrics, there was something to celebrate, if not the architecture itself.

→ New electric trains on BR Southern Region's Kent coast services from 1959 meant these English bathing belles could spend an extra half hour or so sunning themselves on the beaches at Margate, Ramsgate and Broadstairs. The sunny nature, and message, of this Carry On film-style poster belies the shadow of the package holiday by jet charter, which was about to sweep these young ladies away from the Kent coast and off to Costa Brava no matter how fast the new trains.

An artist's impression of the new Piccadilly Station and office block in Manchester now under construction

MANCHESTER'S NEW STATION

Plan of site station showing new platform arrangement

replacing London Road Station will be completed in 1962. More platforms giving better services, easier access and more car parking space are but some of the improvements which will come from this rebuilding

London Midland Modernisation

BRITISH RAILWAYS

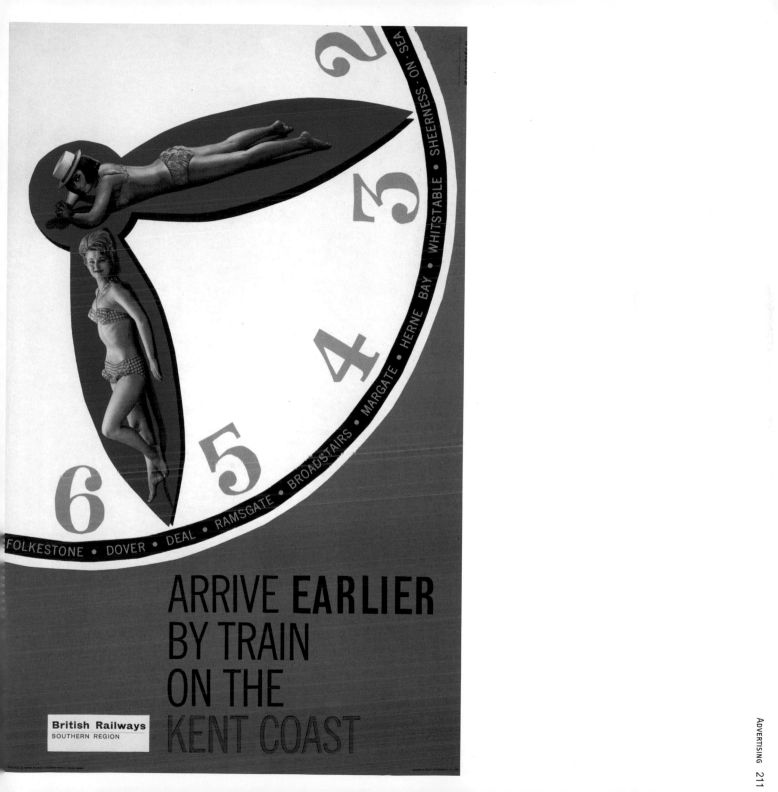

ARRIVE **EARLIER**
BY TRAIN
ON THE
KENT COAST

British Railways
SOUTHERN REGION

↓ British Rail, styled in 1965, was British Railways brought into a world of rapidly expanding car ownership, rampant consumerism and a need to woo backpassengers who had abandoned trains over the previous decade. A snappy new double-arrow logo, Jock Kinneir's Rail Alphabet typeface and the Inter-City brand were essential props for the new-look railway. This ad from the mid-1970s shows what a train could do for you – meet loved ones – rather than what it looked like.

↘ There was only one answer to the question posed by this alluring British Rail Inter-City poster of the mid-1970s. This was the age of resolute male chauvinism in advertising, especially for cars, power drills, tools and gadgets. Somehow, though, this golden young lady recalls the innocence of the bathing beauties that British train travellers had been brought up with since the 1920s. She made you smile on a grey day waiting for a train on a suburban platform miles from any beach.

↘↘ Not difficult to guess which British Rail station the Swedish pop group Abba would have been keeping tidy with their mops, brooms and flared trousers in 1975. Abba had a first, and massive, hit with "Waterloo" in 1974, becoming international stars. They were not singing about the London terminus, but British Rail cannily got them to pose for this campaign which was aimed at encouraging a young commuting generation with a relish for burgers and chewing gum to clean up at stations.

→ HST 125 Inter-City trains began running from London Paddington to Bristol in 1976. This young chap, on his way to Weston-super-Mare, perhaps, is playing out a role created in a 1927 Southern Railway poster, "South for Sunshine", in which a small boy looks up admiringly to the driver of a King Arthur 4-6-0 on its way from Waterloo to the south coast. This is a rather nice update of the image of a schoolboy wanting to be an engine driver.

→ → Wonderful Bauhaus-influenced poster for the LNER's non-stop London King's Cross to Edinburgh service, The Flying Scotsman, by A Thompson. This famous train, powered by a Gresley A1 or A3 Pacific, made a magnificent sight, although it was not fast, averaging just 48mph due to a timing agreement with the rival west coast main line from London to Scotland. The poster is a stylish, knowing play on the Southern Railway's charmingly old-school "South for Sunshine" poster of the year before.

Mister– Im going on Holiday on your train cos I know its The quickest.

≢ Inter-City 125   Have a good trip!

LNER

TAKE ME BY THE FLYING SCOTSMAN

LEAVES KING'S CROSS AT 10 A.M. EVERY WEEK·DAY

WITH APOLOGIES TO THE— SOUTHERN RAILWAY

↑ And now for something completely different.... Here is a train being used as an advertisement, in this case for Lux beauty soap. Awaiting departure from Rangoon, Myanmar, in 1996, there is something poignant in the fact that the train blares out its message to the public outside, while, inside, the passengers are Burmese Buddhist monks who are, presumably, indifferent to such worldly ways of cleansing the body, as opposed to the soul. They certainly look detached from their surroundings. The idea of turning trains into billboards has been taken up, sadly, in all too many parts of the world. In earlier days it was enough for a train to advertise itself; today, painted in garish logos, it might be pressed into duty to advertise any number of consumer goods and services. Surprisingly, because its standards of design and decorum are usually high, one of the worst offenders has been Deutsche Bundesbahn; in 2000, 18 of its new 101 class express passenger electric locomotives were painted as headache-inducing adverts for drugs made by Bayer, Aspirin among others. The same year, a further eleven 101s were painted as adverts for German milk, and 21 for German meat.

→ More tasteless railway advertising, from 2003, for a new, faster Eurostar service from Brussels to London in just two hours, 20 minutes. Quite why Queen Elizabeth has been turned into a parody of Marilyn Monroe in her famous air-vent scene from *The Seven Year Itch* is something only Eurocitizens, such as the gentleman passing with an EC umbrella, might be able to explain. The Queen looks to be in pain, as well she might, reduced to such a vapid role. What had been funny with Britain and Eurostar, from its launch in 1994 to 2003, was the fact that the trains had only been able to travel pitifully slowly through Kent on their way to London. So slow, from the perspective of one of the 186mph (300km/h) trains, that it was easy to imagine a man walking in front with a red flag to warn the English that fast and dangerous foreigners were on the way from the Continent to the capital, where Her Majesty herself might be in residence. The idea that the Eurostar train itself might be depicted in all its mercurial glory must never have entered the heads of the advertising agency that designed this Eurotrash jest.

Naar Londen,
sneller dan ooit

216

FILM

Trains and film are an odd couple. The very first film shown to a public audience was of a train arriving at a station (p218), so you would have thought that the relationship had got off to a good start. But as soon as they thought no one was looking too closely, directors began cutting stock footage of trains into their films in cavalier, or Ed Wood, fashion. Sequences of trains from the wrong era and wrong railway were inserted at random. In the otherwise enjoyable Bond film *From Russia with Love* (p230), the *Orient Express* metamorphoses several times. At one point it appears to have been diverted down the Midland main line with a Royal Scot or Patriot 4-6-0 in charge on its way to London. In the 1970s remake of *The Thirty-Nine Steps*, an Edwardian express train steaming through the Scottish heather is hauled by a BR Standard 4MT 4-6-0 built in 1954. Perhaps a time-machine was involved. One can never be sure of a director's intentions.

In recent years, it has been hard to find the exact period train, as most have long been torched. Or political problems have stood in the way of directors' ambitions. When David Lean, an unabashed railway enthusiast, made *Dr Zhivago* (p229), he was unable to film in the Soviet Union. Its government had taken against Boris Pasternak's anti-Soviet novel on which the film was based, and the filming of veteran Tsarist locomotives was banned; they were state secrets.

Films made by amateur railway enthusiasts are, if accurate, often staggeringly boring, with men in wilfully bad clothes droning on about the inside-cylinder dimensions of Bulleid Pacifics, or, if American, simpering on in "Wonderful World of Disney" voiceovers about "faithful old-time steamers". Others, though, enjoy a candid simplicity. I cherish a film made in the 1930s of a journey to Burtonport on the otherwise long-forgotten Burtonport extension of the Londonderry & Lough Swilly Railway in Northern Ireland. The film is silent, but if you know your locomotives, narrow gauge trains and County Donegal, you can conjure the sound track easily enough. You can almost smell the aroma of steam, hot oil, damp cushions stuffed with horsehair, of peat and the Atlantic Ocean.

In 2003, an Irish journalist uncovered the only known film of the idiosyncratic Listowel & Ballybunion monorail railway in southern Ireland. It is just 58 seconds long, yet manages to take viewers on a tour of the parts of the railway you most want to see. The Lumière brothers would be proud of such elegant concision.

Some of the most likeable railway films have been made by neither film studios with famous stars, nor railway buffs with Super-8 cine cameras, but by railway companies themselves or public corporations. The GPO Film Unit's *Night Mail*, of 1936, is a work of art, starring the poetry of W H Auden, the music of Benjamin Britten, Royal Scot 4-6-0 *Seaforth Highlander*, the West Coast Postal from Euston to Glasgow and the men who worked it. It is a film that makes you proud that Britain once had such people and trains in it, and that public corporations were run by managers who believed in something beyond share options, pensions funds, company cars and marketing speak.

Equally, there is *Big Boy*, a joyous, glossy, black and white film made by the Union Pacific Railroad in 1942. Like *Night Mail*, workmen as well as the imposing 4-8-8-4 locomotives are the stars of this riveting public information film. Watch it; it has true style and shows why locomotives and trains are such natural film stars.

The Lumière brothers, Auguste (1862–1954) and Louis (1864–1948), were on holiday in Provence in July 1895 when they filmed this train arriving at La Ciotat station. They had only just invented the movie camera and although this was not their first shoot – that was of workers leaving their factory earlier in the year – the 50-second *Arrivée d'un Train à La Ciotat* was the first film ever seen by a cinema audience. This event took place in the Grand Café, Boulevard de Capucines on December 28, 1895. The sight of the train drawing ever closer to the screen prompted a number of the specially invited audience to duck behind their seats. From then on, there was no stopping early film makers from working with trains. Although trains moved uncomfortably quickly for the first cameras, they offered guaranteed excitement on film. The Wright Brothers had yet to develop and fly their powered aircraft, and cars were still slow, primitive things, so trains were a symbol of speed, power and progress. The Lumière brothers' train itself is a glorious thing, headed by a characterful, tall-chimneyed locomotive, almost baroque in style with its domes and extravagant architecture. Passengers look appropriately respectful.

↓ *The General* (Clyde Bruckmann and Buster Keaton, 1927) starred the deadpan comedian Buster Keaton as Johnnie Gray, a Confederate railroad engineer. Highly acclaimed today, this silent-era blockbuster was considered overly long when first released; takings were disappointing. The screenplay was based on a real episode from 1861 during the American Civil War, with fictional twists and turns, and nerve-racking stunts like this one, when a real train was crashed off a bridge, in one take. A posse of Union soldiers, in disguise, hijacks a Confederate train at Marietta, Georgia, with, unknown to Johnnie, his true love, Annabelle Lee, aboard. The locomotive is the *General*, a classic American-type 4-4-0. Johnnie gives chase on the line to Chattanooga, and back, at the controls of another 4-4-0, the *Texas*. After convoluted scrapes, Johnnie returns with Annabelle and the *General* to reveal, and foil, dastardly Yankee plans. In reality, the Union raiders were arrested by Confederate soldiers and hung as spies. The real *General*, which did not feature in the film, was built by Rogers, Ketchum & Grosvenor of Paterson, New Jersey, for the Western & Atlantic Railroad, 1855. She last ran in Kentucky in 1966 and is on display at the Southern Museum of Locomotive History, Kennesaw, Georgia.

↑   Jean Gabin, starring as the psychotic *mécanicien* (engine driver) Jacques Lantier in *La Bête Humaine* (Jean Renoir, 1938), leans moodily from the cab of his Chapelon Pacific. This brooding, highly political film was based on Emile Zola's novel of 1890. It tells the story of Lantier, who, prone to blackouts, is caught in a web of murderous deceit. Filmed between Paris and Le Havre, this powerful pyschological thriller is also one of the best railway films ever made. Lantier's loves are a pouting beauty, Severine, played by Simone Simon, and the ficitional *La Lison*, on film a peerless André Chapelon compound Pacific.

↗   This is the Aberdonian express thundering along an embankment on its way north from King's Cross in 1936. It is being filmed as part of one of the longest sequences of *Night Mail*, even though that train – the West Coast Postal – ran from Euston behind a quite different type of locomotive. Sequences of locomotives and trains from other railways, however, have long been used in films featuring railways. For many directors, it is not accuracy that counts, but mood. And, no one can doubt that the footage of this Gresley Pacific in action will make a magnificent spectacle.

→   *Elizabethan Express* (Tony Thompson, 1954) is a handsome, lively 20-minute film made by British Transport Films to celebrate what was then the world's longest non-stop train, the *Elizabethan*, running the 393 miles from London King's Cross to Edinburgh Waverly in six and a half hours at an average speed of 60mph. The film stars everyone involved in making this demanding run possible. Mostly, though, it starred streamlined Gresley A4 Pacific *Silver Fox*, which had once topped 113mph at the head of a regular express. Here, the film crew poses during a break from filming cutaways with sister A4 locomotive *Golden Fleece* at London's Marylebone station.

Overleaf left ←←
Oh Mr Porter! (Marcel Varnel,
1938) is a delightful, bumbling
comedy starring potty Will Hay
(1888–1949) as William Porter, a
wheel-tapper at King's Cross
(pictured with a brand new A4
Pacific) appointed station master
at remote Buggleskelly, Northern
Ireland. Chaos ensues, along with
a ghost train, IRA gun runners and
other diversions. Buggleskelly
was, in reality, Chiddesden Halt
on the abandoned Basingstoke—
Alton branch, southern England.
The train that runs up and down
through the antique station is,
wittily, pulled by a tiny Hawthorn
Leslie 2-4-0T designed by Colonel
Stephens for use on light railways
in 1899; the polar opposite of an
LNER A4.

Overleaf right ←←
Alec: "You know what's happened,
don't you?"
Laura: "Yes, yes, I do."
Alec: "I've fallen in love with you."
Laura: "Yes, I know."
This doomed and less than
steamy, yet movingly
understated, love affair between
a middle-class housewife (Celia
Johnson) and a married doctor
(Trevor Howard) was played out
at a railway junction. She goes
one way, to Ketchworth, he
another, to Churley, while
express trains that represent
their dream of a life together race
heedlessly through the station
and into the dark. Filmed at
Carnforth, Lancashire, *Brief
Encounter* (David Lean, 1945) is
one of the finest English films.

↑   Conversations in dining cars
feature in numerous films. This is
one of the best. In *Strangers on a
Train* (Alfred Hitchcock, 1951),
amateur tennis player Guy Haines
(Farley Granger) meets Bruno
Anthony (Robert Walker), a
charming psychopath, on a New
York to Washington express. An
idle conversation over lunch
between these two young bucks
about a perfect double murder
leads to the inevitable Hitchcock
nightmare. Clothes, table layouts,
trains, and architecture – Penn
Station, New York (p128) is one of
the stars of the film – all play their
part in shaping a glamorous rail-
bound world thundering into a
psychological hell.

→   *Lion*, an 0-4-2 built by Todd
Kitson & Laird of Leeds for the
Liverpool and Manchester
Railway in 1838, served for many
decades as a pump engine at
Prince's Dock, Liverpool. She was
rescued by enthusiasts and
restored, by the LMS, at Crewe, in
time for the 100th anniversary
celebrations of the Liverpool and
Manchester. She appeared, in
steam, in several films, most
famously in *The Titfield
Thunderbolt* (Charles Crichton,
1953), an Ealing Comedy about
villagers determined to re-open
and run their ever-so-English
branch line. In this scene, the
villagers abduct *Thunderbolt*
(*Lion*) from the town museum
(Imperial College, London).

← Marilyn Monroe (as Sugar Kane Kowalczyk) wiggling along the platform at Chicago to board the overnight train to Palm Beach. "Look how she moves," says Jack Lemmon's character, Jerry, in drag as Daphne, "like Jell-O on springs. She must have some sort of built-in motor. I tell you, it's a whole different sex." This scene is taken from *Some Like it Hot* (Billy Wilder, 1959), the much-loved comedy starring Monroe, Lemmon and Tony Curtis. It's 1929; Joe (Curtis) and Jerry (Lemmon) are escaping the Chicago Mob. Dressed as two rather unconvincing ladies (Josephine and Daphne), they escape by joining the all-girl jazz band Sweet Sue's Society Syncopators on the long, steamy ride to

Florida. On board, the open-plan Pullman cars, with their curtained sleeping booths, allowed Wilder a lot of fun filming with the band playing, as bands rarely do on real trains, and as the Beatles were to in *A Hard Day's Night* (Dick Lester, 1964), one of a number of films that borrowed Wilder's train sequence. Steam trains make jazz sounds and run to jazz rhythms, so it was a double-plus for Wilder to set some of movie's paciest scenes on board a syncopating night train.

↓ "I'm Eve Kendall. I'm 26 and unmarried. Now you know everything." "Tell me. What do you do besides lure men to their doom on the *Twentieth Century Limited*?" "I'm an industrial designer." The drop-dead gorgeous Eva Marie Saint as Eve Kendall, a double agent, sharing a sleeping compartment and clever dialogue with Cary Grant's suave New York advertising agent, Roger O Thornhill, mistaken for a secret agent, and set up for murder. The plot of *North by Northwest* (Alfred Hitchcock, 1959) gets a lot more complicated before the *Twentieth Century Limited*, with these two star-crossed lovers aboard, rolls into La Salle Street, Chicago. Hitchcock used the real New York Central

train for much of these rail-bound sequences. This was the diesel-hauled version that went into service in 1948; like its fabulous 1938 streamlined steam-hauled predecessor, it was designed by an industrial designer, Henry Dreyfuss. The sleeping compartments were equipped with private showers and lavatories, the restaurant car offered choice food and cocktails (Grant's character opts for a Gibson), and Hitchcock made brilliant use of the stylish train. Within a few years of the film's premiere, this train, and others like it, would be killed off by airlines.

← The construction of the 415km Thai–Burma railway – the "Death Railway" was an act of sheer barbarity. Three hundred thousand Allied soldiers, and local people, were starved and otherwise killed by the Japanese imperial army during the Second World War to clear the line through south-east Asian jungle and, famously, over the River Kwai at Kanchanaburi, 50 miles west of Bangkok. The railway was made famous by *The Bridge over the River Kwai* (David Lean, 1957), a stirring if fictional account: the actual bridge was destroyed by Allied bombing and not by actor William Holden. The present day structure is prosaic.

↑ A scene of the highest, and some say campest, drama: the circus train crashes in *The Greatest Show on Earth* (Cecil B DeMille, 1952). James Stewart, dressed as a clown, saves the life of the circus boss, played by Charlton Heston; Stewart's clown is in fact a top surgeon wanted for murder. If this sounds unreal, so was the train. The crash sequence was filmed using model trains. It is well done, though, and is the best remembered scene of this love-it-or-hate-it epic. Shots of lions, monkeys and other animals roaming about after the derailment were superimposed.

↑↑ Not exactly keen on Boris Pasternak's anti-Soviet novel, *Dr Zhivago*, Moscow refused to allow the story to be filmed in the USSR. The extensive train sequences of the Oscar-winning epic *Dr Zhivago* (David Lean, 1965), starring Omar Sharif and Julie Christie, were filmed in Finland and Canada, where snow, lakes and forests abound and steam trains are at their most picturesque. Elsewhere, Spain, smothered in fake snow, stood in for the former Soviet Union. This train is steaming across a vast Rockies landscape. The log-built station featured extensively in the film is Lake Louise station, Banff, British Columbia.

↑ The Hejaz Railway, built by the German engineer Heinrich Meissner on behalf of the Turks, was paid for by Muslims worldwide. Opened in 1913, this pilgrim route got as far south as Medina, 1,320km from its starting point, Damascus. A journey that had previously taken two months by camel train now took 55 hours. During the First World War, T E Lawrence, a British officer, led the Arab Revolt against the Turks, who used the railway as a supply line. His legendary exploits were recreated at original locations in Jordan in *Lawrence of Arabia* (David Lean, 1962), a screen epic starring Peter O'Toole.

←   James Bond (Sean Connery) has escaped from Istanbul on the *Orient Express* with Tatiana Romanova (Daniela Bianchi). At Zagreb they are joined at dinner by SPECTRE assassin Donald Grant (Robert Shaw) posing as 007's British contact Captain Nash. Nash spikes Tatiana's glass of Taittinger champagne. All three retire to Bond's compartment... Tatiana swoons; Bond is knocked on the head by Grant. Only when he comes to, at gunpoint, does he realize that he should have known their dining companion was no good: Grant had chosen a Chianti – red wine – to accompany his grilled sole. *From Russia with Love* (Terence Young, 1963).

↑   When the film version of Agatha Christie's *Murder on the Orient Express* (Sidney Lumet, 1974) was made, the *Orient Express* was a shadow of its former self. Parts of old carriages were brought to the film studios to recreate the train in its 1934 heyday. It looked good. Here, with the train stuck in snow, the Belgian dectective Hercule Poirot (Albert Finney) interviews a star-studded cast of possible murderers. The scenes depicting the train on the move were consistent, unlike those in *From Russia with Love*, in which archive film of 1960s British steam trains were worked unconvincingly into the mix.

↑ 3am, August 8, 1963, Sears Crossing, Buckinghamshire. The Glasgow to London overnight TPO (Travelling Post Office) train is brought to a halt by an unexpected red signal. A gang of 15 villains cosh driver Jack Mills and get away with £2.6 million in cash. Although the robbers were caught, over many years in some cases, and Mills never recovered from his beating, the gang passed into English folklore, like some latter-day version of Robin Hood's Merry Men. A film – *Robbery* (Peter Yates, 1967) – was made of the story, but with its cast of sharp suits and dodgy gor' blimey accents, it was not a patch on the real event. TPOs vanished from the British railway scene, sorely missed, in 2004.

↗ Filmed on the preserved Keighley and Worth Valley Railway, Yorkshire, the film version of E Nesbit's *The Railway Children* (Lionel Jeffries, 1970) has been one of the most popular and enduring of all British children's films. The Edwardian children, led by eldest sister Bobby (Jenny Agutter), and their mother are forced to live a life of humble rural poverty after their father is wrongly imprisoned as a spy. They befriend an important railway director, whom they wave to innocently each day as this rather unconvincing "express" train, drawn by a Lancashire and Yorkshire Railway 0-6-0, built for freight services in 1887, ambles by. Their "Old Gentleman" helps free father. Bobby meets him on the platform. "Daddy! My Daddy," she cries. Audiences dissolved into tears as credits rolled.

→ *Trainspotting* (Danny Boyle, 1996) is a dark, cynical, funny Scottish film about a group of boys who live for sex, drugs and more drugs. It is not about trainspotting in the accepted meaning of the word, but it does suggest, as pictured here, that life can go on and off the rails, and that there is always another line in life to travel down. You can mainline, or turn off at a junction and take a slower route altogether. The music tracks were by Pulp, Damon Albarn of Blur and Leftfield. Blur produced an album, *Modern Life is Rubbish*, featuring streamlined Gresley A4 Pacific *Mallard* on the sleeve; perhaps there was some real trainspotting in the world of sex, drugs and rock'n'roll after all.

234 PEOPLE

In 1964, Ian Allan published a biography of Bill Hoole. It sold out. Bill who? "Engineman extraordinary" is what it said on the cover. The reader was not cheated. Bill Hoole was one of England's favourite engine drivers. He was a celebrity of sorts. Enthusiasts knew that Hoole would always try and make up time if, for any reason, the train he was driving was late. He ran as fast as it was safe to on the Eastern Region of British Railways in the 1950s, and became, like Casey Jones, something of a folk hero, although he was neither celebrated in song nor in a weekly TV show.

When he retired, in 1959, Hoole and his wife moved from north London to north Wales, so that he could take up a job as an engine driver on the narrow-gauge Ffestiniog Railway. He kept at this until he died in his early eighties.

"Imagine publishing a best-selling biography of an engine driver today," exclaimed Ian Allan when I interviewed him for *The Observer* in 2004. "No one would be interested unless the chap happened to be a part-time mad-axe murderer."

Yet, once upon a time, countless thousands of young boys had wanted to be engine drivers when they grew up. In 2004, they wanted to be football stars, rap stars, TV stars or just generally rich, famous, loud and bad. Greed was good, shopping a religion. Public service and civic duty sucked.

What had happened along the way? Much depends on the country where you live. In Britain and the United States, the status of railways and railway workers was reduced and denigrated from the 1960s. This was sad for, on the whole, they have been a proud bunch, with important and highly responsible jobs whether in blue or white collar employment.

A successful railway is a network, or system, that requires every employee from porter to Pullman car attendant, signalman to senior executive, driver to diesel mechanic, to pull his or her weight. Which is why a top-link engine driver like Bill Hoole was as important as Sir Nigel Gresley, the engineer who designed the A4 locomotives Hoole drove to such great effect, and anyone else along the lines he sped, from the station announcer at King's Cross to wheel-tappers at Doncaster.

Railways had been a calling for many people. They went to work for them in their mid-teens, whether as engine cleaners or engineering apprentices, and stayed with them to retirement. Sons would follow fathers. Skills would be handed down and added to through generations.

At times, the railways resembled religions. Victorian locomotive superintendents, for example, were veritable god-like figures. Their locomotives made railways; they were often the public face of the companies they served. Inevitably, then, railways produced imperious and sometimes eccentric figures whose word was law, even when it was clearly wrong. I love reading about the ascetic and rather frightening Frances Webb, chief locomotive superintendent of the London and North Western Railway. He did design some splendid engines, like the nimble Precedent, or "Jumbo", 2-4-0s of 1874. Equally, he was responsible for one dud class of compound express passenger locomotive after another; the driving wheels of his Dreadnought and Teutonic 2-2-2-0s would slip in opposite directions while they debated which way the train should go. Yet no one dared question fierce Frances Webb. He died in office. His successor, George Whale, was, thankfully, a genial fellow as well as a robust and practical designer. Yes, it might be a cliché, but railways, because they have often been self-contained worlds, have produced their fair share of remarkable characters.

↖ Here is *Fräuenfeld*, a Swiss 4-4-0 designed for crossing the mountainous border with Austria, in 1854. "Fräuenfeld" means field of women but, as you can see, this impeccable locomotive is surrounded by no fewer than 22 men, and not a single fräu in sight. She will be back home at this early stage in railway history, preparing the enginemen's bath and supper. Early railway photographers were familiar with this situation: as soon as they were about to take a picture of a locomotive, a crowd of fierce-looking men – hands on hips, chimneys and handbrakes – would appear as if from nowhere. Photography was still very much a novelty, as was the express passenger train; they more or less

developed together. This highly posed photograph reveals, proudly, the sheer number of men, from coal heavers, cleaners and mechanics, to drivers, firemen and military-style inspectors, needed to prepare a locomotive like *Fräuenfeld*.

← The railroad played a key role in the American Civil War, a war designed, in part, to free Negroes from slavery. For all the noble talk of equality, life, liberty and the pursuit of happiness, many black workers found themselves poorly treated and poorly paid in the North after hostilities ended in 1865. No question here as to who are the bosses and who the navvies. Two stern-looking bearded foremen in thick, blue military coats pose with two beardless black navvies for a photographer working on behalf of the United States Military Railway Service in the early 1860s. The location is northern Virginia. It was navvies, or "navigators", who sweated blood to build the world's railways.

↑ California, 1890s. Here a self-confident young dude in starched white shirt, waistcoat and fob watch strikes a proprietorial attitude while a gang of three Chinese coolies freeze at the controls of a hand-powered trolley. Thousands of cheap Chinese immigrants were employed by railroads on the west coast of the United States to do the toughest jobs. The big change since is that the Chinese now stay at home to do the developed world's harder tasks, while they have been more than busy building their own railways across deserts, mountains and river valleys, as challenging as any landscape California had to offer a

century ago. The hand-trolley itself is a neat demonstration of how railways triumphed over traffic drawn by horses along uncertain roads in the 19th century: just two 0.1hp men can propel themselves along tracks almost as fast as a horse by employing little energy and the simplest possible mechanism.

↑　A guard gives passengers a warning, and engine crew the "right of way", by blowing a whistle and waving a green flag, a scene played out on railways worldwide. This fierce-looking chap with a beard (so many of these in Victorian photographs) is in charge of a London and North Western Railway boat express, connecting with ships from Ireland, leaving Holyhead on its way to London Euston in 1895. His uniform is, of course, immaculate, as is the "plum and spilt milk" livery of the First Class saloon car behind him. The locomotive, out of sight at the head of the train, painted in deep coats of "blackberry black", will be as polished as the guard's boots; he has every right to look proud.

↗　"You can clip my ticket any time, young miss." "Lawks, sir, I don't know to what you are referring." The Ancient Railwayman stops a young lady ticket inspector at a platform along the Great Central Railway's Manchester to London Marylebone main line during the First World War (1914–18). With so many young men sent away for slaughter in the trenches of France and Belgium, British women took on many railway jobs, and proved themselves every bit as competent as the men they replaced. The Great Central was itself a young railway; it reached London, the last main line to do so, in 1899. It was also, sadly, the first to go, in 1966, by which time this young lady would have been in her eighties.

→　Glamorous young lady guard, in high, laced boots and cap set at a jaunty angle, waves her train away from a station on the Metropolitan Railway, London, during the First World War. Women performed many roles on the wartime railways, but when peace came most went back to housework, domestic service, or jobs in shops and factories. The electric train – as witnessed by the manually operated sliding door of the guard's compartment, the semaphore signal and milk churns at the end of the platform – was hard at work in a world of mechanical operation, steam, men-know-best, Victorian agriculture and trench warfare. This train was built just before the war for the Metropolitan's Uxbridge branch, electrified in 1906. Regular steam services continued on the Metropolitan until 1961.

Overleaf left ← ← Fellow travellers on the world's railways have long included rats. Millions of the disease-carrying rodents. Here cloth-capped Jim Forty and Alfred Greenwin display the traps and poisons of their trade at St Pancras goods yard, London in the early 1930s. Their canine companions, Jill, Sally and Tint are, of course, the real rat catchers. They look very pleased with the results of a morning's work, the corpses of at least a dozen Cockney rats. What they would have been unable to catch were the fleas that sometimes bothered passengers on sultry days, but that is another, itchy, tale.

Overleaf right ← ← *American Gothic*, Chicago Northwestern Railroad style, Wilmette, Illinois, 1930. The Great Depression has made millions redundant; labour is dispensable, but not so dispensable that the railroad can afford to lose crossing guards to errant motorists. This mournful fellow, with his whistle, natty tie and stop-sign lollipop, sports a new railroad-issue red and white striped belt; this is to make him visible to drivers racing trains to rural crossings. Today, no one could miss him. In an age of statutory baseball caps, trainers and leisurewear, such a well-dressed railway worker holding down such a menial job would cause passers-by to stop.

↑ "Sorry, ma'am, you've just missed Toronto; 'fraid Vancouver is your next station stop." A smartly uniformed train conductor checking tickets on board a Canadian National Railways express, circa 1948. This was an era in which staff as well as passengers, like these fine-hatted ladies, dressed up to travel by train. Within 20 years, as long distances were made increasingly by airline jets, the standards of passenger trains in North America and parts of Europe, notably Great Britain, began to decline. Smart, authoritative, military-style uniforms gave way to egg-stained slob gear, while passengers became "customers", continuously eating, and dressed and acting like yobs.

↗ When steam Pullman services on the London to Brighton line gave way to electric on January 1, 1933, the name of the prestigious *Southern Belle* was changed to *Brighton Belle*. In this Southern Railway publicity shot, a year later, station staff at Victoria, London, make a play of swapping the Pullman train's nameboards. The crew of the 5-BEL EMU peek out over the Brighton coat-of-arms. The train's First Class coaches bore such everyday names as *Doris*, *Audrey* and *Vera*, but took such eminent passengers as Laurence Olivier up to town, and the stage, from his south coast home. This was the only train of its type in the world; it was much missed by thespians and railwaymen alike when it was withdrawn in 1972.

→ Lord Street station, Southport, Lancashire, January 7, 1952. The last train has left, and the station is about to be closed for good. Smartly dressed staff take down the "finger board" signs ("it's rude to point," said schoolchildren, jokingly) which announced Manchester and Aintree expresses, and a local train to Knotty Ash. Many of Britain's railway stations were to go the same way a decade later when, in 1963, the Beeching Report recommended the closure of thousands of miles of railways that, unprofitable then, would be a godsend in today's traffic-crowded island. Quite why the staff are so cheerful is a mystery.

Overleaf left ←← The *Royal Scot* was a distinguished train. Here it is, in 1956, preparing to depart London Euston, at 10am sharp, for its run to Glasgow Central. Harry Turrell, Euston station master, in top hat, button hole and tails, is here to see the express away. The crew are: locomotive inspector Sam Smith of Rugby, in trilby hat; driver Gray, on the platform; and fireman Moffat leaning from the footplate window. Gray and Moffat are from Upperby shed, Carlisle, 300 miles north of London. Their mount is one of the magnificent Stanier Princess Coronation, four-cylinder Pacifics, 46240 *City of Coventry*. Lucky men.

Overleaf right ←← "I 'ear yer still livin' in Beffnal Green and playin' football, me ol' China?" "Yer, squire, as ver 'istory books tell us, we won't be movin' aht to Essex and playin' golf for anovvah 25 bleedin' years." Cockney Pete'n'Dud-style London taxi drivers lean on the bonnet of one of a row of spotless FX3 and FX4 cabs, Euston station, February 1960. Within five years, the FX3 cabs will have largely gone, along with not only the steam trains serving Euston, but the station itself. In 1961, its famous arch (p.126) was demolished. In 1965, electric trains took over main line as well as local services, and in 1968, the new Euston station was opened by the Queen; it looked exactly like an airport terminal.

↑ Trainspotters have long been part and parcel of Britain's railways. Here, a pair of standard-issue schoolboy enthusiasts lean over the wall of a bridge to watch a Stanier 8F 2-8-0 steam beneath them, Lancashire, 1967. This was a year before the end of regular main line steam working in Britain. Many trainspotters moved on to other pursuits, yet there were those who continued to stand at platform ends, in weather foul and fair, duffle bags laden with Ian Allan *Locospotter's Guides*, fishpaste sandwiches and Penguin biscuits. Railways were not the same without steam, but enthusiasts who simply liked collecting locomotive numbers barely noticed the changeover to diesel and electric traction.

→ Behind the scenes, the steam railway loved by enthusiasts was not quite so glamorous as they wanted it to be. Here, Jamaican men, newly arrived in London, shovel soot, clinker, smut and cinders from a trough between the tracks at Old Oak Common motive power depot, west of Paddington station. A Collett Castle Class 4-6-0 simmers in the background; it will have generated a good deal of this detritus on its fast run out to Worcester and back at the head of the *Cathedrals Express*. Colin T Gifford's chiaroscuro study of steam, soot and graft captures a time when such dirty work fell to immigrants from the West Indies and Indian sub-continent as established residents moved on to diesel-age jobs with their promise of clean collars and ties. For all their grime, though, such engine sheds were haunting and romantic places, choc full, in this case, of generations of handsome former Great Western Railway locomotives, Kings and Castles among them. Many were kept in good condition to the last and remained quite able to run diesel-age trains timed at a mile-a-minute and more at up to 100mph. Steam services to Paddington ended in 1965. So did these jobs.

↓ Steam men at work in the heat of the Bengal plains. This is one of the tiny 0-4-0 tank locomotives of the Darjeeling Railway being being serviced at Siliguri. This ritual continues into the twenty-first century. The cab of a steam locomotive can be almost unbearably hot in such conditions but, once on the move, the slightest slipstream will cool down a footplate open to the elements like this. And then it is a pleasure.

↘ In time honoured fashion, a boiler-suited driver oils the motion of Ferrocarril Nacional 3826, an oil-burning class 12B 4-6-0 . First built as compounds in 1906, these Argentinian locomotives had long and useful lives. In the US and other advanced steam countries, locomotives were able to oil themselves. Still, there can be something enjoyable in pottering about while tending the motion of a steam locomotive; rather like watering prize roses, but not on a rainy day.

→ Late flowering steam men, Calcutta, 1996. These labourers are employed shovelling coal from a coal train into lorries for local distribution. By this time, Indian railways had effectively abandoned steam, if not coal. Steam stayed late in India because of the country's abundant supplies of coal and cheap labour. Yet the world of these men was changing; today, they could just as well be working in a call centre, answering enquiries from British train passengers.

↘↘ Late flowering steam men, Xingyang, 2002. The only little red books these men in blue boiler suits carry are books of railway rules and regulations. The steam locomotive continues, hard at work, in the People's Republic of China on a number of heavy-duty, and narrow-gauge, freight lines, notably in Inner Mongolia. These men are working SY 2-8-2 1406, one of a class of shunting and industrial locomotives built from 1969, at the Shangjie Aluminium Works.

Overleaf left →→ Working class hero. A study of a Top Link (Eastern Region, British Railways) driver at the throttle of an A1 Pacific, at speed, in the late 1950s. Unlike racing drivers who peak in their 20s and 30s, these iron-road jockeys reached the summit of their highly skilled careers in their 50s and early 60s. One of these East Coast main-line drivers, Bill Hoole, was the subject of a full length biography .

Overleaf right →→ In stark contrast, here is the driver of a 300kph Eurostar at the controls of his 18-car electric express. Dressed in a natty polyester-nylon suit, he could be the manager of a call centre rather than the driver of such a prestigious train.

INDEX

CREDITS

The publishers would like to thank the following sources for their kind permission to reproduce the pictures in the book.

AKG London: 47
Alvey & Tower: 77b
© Archives/Photorail/Diaporama: 209r
© ARRPI/Photorail/Diaporama: 31
Robin Barnes: 171b
Brienz Rothorn Railway: 150b
British Film Institute: 221, 223
© Broncard/Photorail/Diaporama: 41b
Canada Science and Technology Museum Corporation: 62r, 77, 80t, 100bl, 191r, 195bl, 241b
Corbis: 128, 130, 174, 177, 189, 200l, 229br, 236b; /Austrian Archive: 236t; Neil Beer: 136b; /Yann Arthus Bertrand: 137; /Bettmann: 66, 86r, 87, 92br, 94bl, 94br, 94tl, 96b, 96t, 98, 99, 116, 119, 162l, 163, 166, 170, 180, 187b, 192, 194, 195br, 196, 197, 200r, 241tr; /Dean Conger: 100br, 100tr; /Own Franken: 171t; /Marc Garanger: 135; /Historical Picture Archive: 104tr; /Robert Holmes: 131; /

Jeremy Horner: 249t; /Dave G. Houser: 76; /Hulton-Deutsch Collection:36, 49, 53, 88, 91r, 92bl, 92t, 93, 94tr, 108-109,162r, 186, 187t, 188, 240; /K J Historical: 202r, 204, 205r, 209l; /Chris Lisle: 214; /Medford Historical Society: 175t, 175b; /Colin Garratt/Milepost 92 1/2: 148; /Minnesota Historical Society: 46b; Kelly Mooney Photography: 129; / Nasa: 120-121; /Matthew Polak: 118; / Charles E Rotkin: 67; /Rykoff Collection: 167; /Schenectady Museum: 61, 64; /Phil Schermeister: 136t; /Setboun: 133, 138-139; /Joseph Sohm: 195; /Hubert Stadler: 151; /Swim Ink: 201l, 202l, 203, 205l, 205c, 208, 210; /Ruet Stephane: 139; /Underwood & Underwood: 237, 238r; /Michael S Yamashita: 101; / Miroslav Zajic: 100tl
© DR/Photorail/Diaporama: 65
Getty Images: Hulton Archive: 6, 29, 33t, 40, 43l, 43r, 44, 60, 69, 86l, 104b, 111b, 115, 117b, 153, 159b, 161, 164b, 164t, 178l, 178r, 179, 181t, 181b, 220r, 243l
Colin T. Gifford: 54, 55, 244, 247
Imperial War Museum: 182, 183, 190, 193
Lonely Planet Images: Diana Mayfield:

78-79
Milepost 92 1/2: 32, 34-35, 37, 38t, 42, 44-45, 46t, 48, 51, 56-57, 72, 73, 80tl, 81, 82, 83r, 83l, 149t, 158, 169; /Colin Garratt: 50, 248l, 248r, 249b; /M G Gatow: 147; /R S Carpenter: 110; /Mike Satow: 62tl; / Ron Ziel: 146
Millbrook House Limited: 71, 73, 74r, 74l, 80br, 80bl, 144, 145b, 149br; Hugh Ballantyne: 155t, 155b; A.W. Croughton: 143; /National Railway Museum/E. Treacy: 68t, 250-251; /J.T. Shaughnessy: 68b; /Southern Pacific Historical Collection: 159t; S.C.Townroe: 165; /C.M.Whitehouse: 149bl, 150t
Photos12.com: 220l, 224; /Societe Francaise de Photographie: 117t
Picture Desk: 206l, 206r, 207l, 207r, 226, 229t
Reuters Limited: 215
Rex Features: Roger Viollet: 132
Romney Hythe & Dymchurch LRC: Courtesy of Peter Rothschild OBE,TD: 152
Ronald Grant Archive: 218, 219, 222, 225, 227, 228, 229bl, 230, 231, 232, 233t, 233b
Santa Maria Novella Station: 134

Science & Society: 30b, 30t, 89, 91l, 97, 104tl, 105, 111t, 112, 113, 114, 124-125, 127, 142, 160, 191l, 201r, 211, 212l, 212c, 213l, 213r, 245; /Daily Herald Archive/ NMPFT: 154, 238l; /National Railway Museum: 28, 33b, 38b, 41t, 52, 62bl, 63, 70, 90, 95, 145t, 168, 184, 184-185 239, 241tl, 242, 243r
Topham Picturepoint: 10, 39, 107, 176; / Novosti: 106
Upmain: 251

Every effort has been made to acknowledge correctly and contact the source and/or copyright holder of each picture. Carlton Books Limited apologizes for any unintentional errors or omissions, which will be corrected in future editions of this book.